# Boy Crazy!

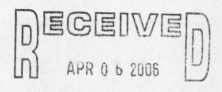

**Also by Charlene C. Giannetti and Margaret Sagarese**

*The Roller-Coaster Years*

*Parenting 911*

*The Patience of a Saint*

*Cliques*

*What Are You Doing in There?*

*Good Parents, Tough Times*

# BOY CRAZY!

## Keeping Your Daughter's
## Feet on the Ground
## When Her Head
## Is in the Clouds

Charlene C. Giannetti

*and*

Margaret Sagarese

Broadway Books

*New York*

BROADWAY

Broadway Books titles may be purchased for business or promotional use or for
special sales. For information, please write to: Special Markets Department,
Random House, Inc., 1745 Broadway, New York, NY 10019.

PRINTED IN THE UNITED STATES OF AMERICA

BROADWAY BOOKS and its logo, a letter B bisected on the diagonal,
are trademarks of Random House, Inc.

Visit our Web site at www.broadwaybooks.com

First edition published 2006

Book design by Patrice Sheridan

Library of Congress Cataloging-in-Publication Data
Giannetti, Charlene C.
Boy crazy! : keeping your daughter's feet on the ground when her head is in the
clouds / by Charlene C. Giannetti and Margaret Sagarese.— 1st ed.
p.   cm.
1. Parent and teenager.   2. Teenage girls—Psychology.   3. Preteens—Psychology.
4. Love in adolescence.   5. Daughters.   I. Sagarese, Margaret.   II. Title.
HQ799.15.G52 2006
306.7'0835'2—dc22                    2005044295

ISBN 0-7679-1976-9

1   3   5   7   9   10   8   6   4   2

To Denise Marcil, a long overdue thank-you

# Contents

# Acknowledgments

*Boy Crazy!* is our sixth book for the parents of young and older adolescents, and we couldn't have completed it without the help of so many people. We'd like to take a moment to thank them.

Our gratitude goes out to all the parents, administrators, educators, and adolescents who volunteered their time to meet with us in focus groups, write to us, or answer our surveys. Talking about romantic issues is highly sensitive and so we appreciate the honesty and courage you all exhibited.

We thank the National Middle School Association, especially John Lounsbury, Sue Swaim, Jack Berckemeyer, and Doug Herlensky for their ongoing dedication to middle school children and for supporting our efforts and helping us continue to reach a network of educators in the United States and Canada.

A word of appreciation goes out to the National PTA, particularly to Joan Kuersten, editor at *Our Children* magazine, who keeps us in touch with parents through this incredible network.

This book would not be as lively and entertaining if it were not for the creative touch of our editor, Patricia Medved, senior editor at Broadway Books. Thank you, Trish, for carefully analyzing our manuscript and guiding us toward changing things for the better. The word *rewrite* is rarely wlecomed, but in this case the extra work definitely enhanced our goal. Beth Datlowe, assistant editor, took time to fine-tune the final copy. Along the way she patiently and professionally answered our many queries and requests. Thanks, Beth.

There are many others at Broadway who toil away on our behalf and we wish to mention them: Thanks to Heather Maguire for all her publicity acumen and effort, and to everyone in marketing and sales who works for us.

To our agent, Denise Marcil: if our dedication doesn't say it all, we want to express our affection for you. You have seen us through six books. It always starts with your reaction to our ideas and our book proposals. Without your instinct and wise advice, we never would have so many books to our credit. "Thank you" remains insufficient.

Thanks to our families, our husbands and our children, who have nurtured and inspired us more than we can say.

Finally, a heartfelt thanks to all the parents who come to our presentations, post reviews of our books online, and continue to motivate us by sharing their struggles, concerns, and triumphs. We couldn't do this job without you. Please accept our gratitude. We look forward to meeting you at one of our talks.

# Boy Crazy!

# I'm in the Mood for Love

## *Are You Ready?*

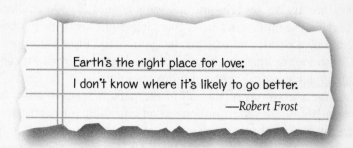

Earth's the right place for love:
I don't know where it's likely to go better.

—*Robert Frost*

Does your daughter seem boy crazy to you? Do you catch your-self thinking: *Whatever happened to my little girl, my carefree, in-nocent eleven-year-old (or twelve-year-old, or thirteen-year-old)?*

Overnight, your little girl has transformed. Yesterday's imp whiled away hours grooming her collection of Barbie dolls or rearranging her soccer patches. Her life was simple. Suddenly, she is complicated. She stares into the mirror or avoids her re-flection altogether. Or she pouts seductively with lips so glossy their sheen is blinding. Her taste in clothing has changed. She picks out tighter tops and low-slung blue jeans. Maybe she cat-walks across her bedroom dressed like Barbie—with big hair and a tiny outfit. Didn't you just see that same look in her *Teen People* magazine? Did her inspiration come from those girls on *The O.C.*?

When her girlfriends arrive, it's as if a Barbie convention convenes. Giggles harmonize with a chorus of cell phones. From her bedroom you catch waves of smells, strawberries and mangoes and perfumes that promise girls they can smell just like J-Lo or Britney or Beyoncé. You overhear "He's so hot!" as if all these girls have taken elocution lessons from Paris Hilton and Nicole Richie. Is this the end of innocence?

You hear other mothers worrying about their daughters, too. There are those who think their girls care too much about getting noticed by the hotties of middle school. But not all mothers are trying to rein in little-girls-gone-wild. Others fret because their little girls aren't changing. Some are being left behind by a best friend who got her period and lusty hormones. These moms whisper about tweenage blues and read articles about adolescent depression more carefully.

The one sentiment that *all* of the parents seem to share is trepidation. They view puberty as an oncoming hurricane that inevitably will thrust many girls into emotional turbulence and romantic tornadoes. *I'm in the mood for love* may be the sound track for ten- to fifteen-year-old girls, but parents are not ready to face that music. Ready or not here it comes.

One cannot blame parents for worrying about whether their daughter seems obsessed with boys or too distressed with the search for romance. Parents are surrounded with boy-crazy warnings. Society and the media play and replay timeless headlines about kids growing up too fast and girls who are out of control and too much into sex. Adolescent love stories published for adult consumption often feature tragic themes, like young lovers who make suicide pacts or a school sniper who goes on a rampage because his heart has been stomped on. Experts offer little in the way of positive information. Every report either warns about the comeback of AIDS or how abstinence from intercourse foments oral sex and anal sex. Memoirs that become bestsellers always seem to retell a former adolescent's story of being promiscuous, smashed, or drugged.

## Timeless Teenagers in Love

Suspend your anxiety for a moment. Think back to when you hovered around puberty. Chances are you can retrieve bitter-sweet sensations with a very mixed heart. Wasn't it a time when you spent most of your daydreams planning and imagining what would, what could happen if he knew how you really felt? Back then anything seemed possible, any happy ending be-tween you and a certain boy was just around the corner. Can you remember how it felt to be naïve and hopeful? Wishing and hoping, and thinking and praying—can you recall the anticipa-tion of romance that directly or indirectly affected everything?

Sweet, yes, but dark memories will come through, too. Who didn't feel lonely and confused much of the time? The face of teen angst had your name attached to it. And even if you had lots of girlfriends and kept busy with activities and schoolwork, what you probably recall as most poignant always revolved around matters of the heart, the sad, and the wistful.

A girl's tween years are tinged by the pursuit of true love. The sweetness and the earnestness of a young girl's quest is a timeless and universal story. The search for true love and the purity of early romantic feelings have spawned so many songs, plays, books, and movies because of their universality. A young girl— the one you once were, the one your daughter is becoming—still recognizes herself in Juliet's longing soliloquy on the balcony.

Can you see the face of your first crush? How old were you? If your experience reflects the majority, you were ten, probably an insecure, knobby-kneed fifth-grader, lusting after the cutest boy in her class. Think of the *Peanuts* cartoon heroine Lucy drooling over Schroeder as he plays his piano. One mother re-members:

His name was Toby. I couldn't stop thinking about him. He had blond hair and the most enormous blue eyes. He didn't know I existed, but that didn't stop me from moon-ing over him. I stared at him in math class, and spent every waking hour scheming to bump into him *acciden-tally.* At the end of the school year at a field day, he gave me a shotgun shell he found on the ball field. I brought it home, polished it, and put it in my keepsake box. Recently, cleaning out a closet, I ran across that box and the shell. Talk about perfect timing! My eleven-year-old is obsessed with a boy in her class. I was obsessed about her obsession! I forgot what that felt like until I discovered that forgotten token of love.

According to University of Michigan's Martha McClintock, professor and chair of the committee on biopsychology, men and women (whether they are heterosexual or homosexual) remember their first love at age ten with the most clarity. Professor McClintock believes that brains imprint those early encounters and make them forever accessible and memorable due to the timing of development along with the power of its hormones. So those longings in middle school remain eternally sharp compared to earlier crushes from sandbox days or later infatuations that are apt to be fuzzy.

As you watch your daughter sucked into the magnetic field of boys and romance, let your own vivid memories wash over you. Recapturing your youth and discovering empathy can make you a more sensitive parent. (You'll see more about how to use memory lane for your daughter's benefit in chapter 3.)

## As Time Goes By

That desire to find love, to fall in love, and to be loved in return remains the same from generation to generation. What has changed is the landscape of young love and the current circumstances that young girls encounter.

At thirteen you may have been swooning in your living room over droopy-eyed Ricky Nelson from the TV show *Ozzie and Harriet.* Or you may have had your ear close to the stereo speakers letting John Lennon's raspy vocals make your loins twist and shout. Or perhaps you longed to jump into the TV so you could be closer to the Partridges (namely Keith) or a Brady Bunch hunk. Compared to those points of reference, it's scary to see your thirteen-year-old watching reruns of Ozzy Osbourne and his clan. TV land and reality TV and movies like *Thirteen* have characters juggling love in tandem with self-mutilation, steroid use, and casual sex without parental supervision anywhere.

You may encounter too many permissive and clueless parents who allow their provocatively clad fashionistas to plot unsupervised rendezvous. Situations arise that your experience has not equipped you to handle confidently. Take this mother's quandary for example: "My daughter's been invited to a coed sleepover birthday party. I don't approve, but apparently I am a minority. The hosting mother says 'don't worry' because the boys and girls will have separate sleeping bags. I ask myself: Have these parents lost their minds? Their kid just turned thirteen!"

As we march into the twenty-first century, what's normal social behavior for a tweenager and what's not? Parents alarmed by the sexually charged culture in which we live have lost sight of absolute rules and answers. Many work themselves up into a fever pitch over a child's first kiss or even the thought of a one-on-one encounter. One mom from Washington, DC, says, "The idea of my fourteen-year-old daughter having a first date turned me upside down. It terrified me. I felt out of control. I called the boy's mother and father. I could hear the mother thinking: 'This woman's insane!' I sounded freaked out, even to myself."

Even though the culture is different, edgier and coarser, and even though you and your daughters have different experiences, you need to focus on the fact that you have a great deal in common. You both want her to blossom into a warm, loving young woman fully capable of a satisfying romantic life. You both want her to become independent and yet remain safe along the way. You both want her to find true love. These goals are shared by moms who wish their daughters would rein in boy-crazy behavior, as well as those parents who pray that their daughters will get a party invitation one of these days.

## The Gift of Romantic Intelligence

We aim to show you how to put your little girl's romantic behavior into the proper context. Out there in the world, it seems all everyone talks about is s-e-x. But there are many other ancillary conversations and accompanying issues that merit your time and attention. As you see us explore various aspects of the social tweenage landscape, you will be better able to help your children cope and enjoy. Your girl's romantic adventures and misadventures, as well as the longings that don't materialize, provide you both with a wealth of opportunities. Your child's "social wish list" is the canvas upon which you can—together—weave insights and restraints. Her wistful, wonderful, heartbreaking, and heavenly experiences provide you with a fertile plain upon which to imprint your values, not a futile wasteland of teenage debauchery and doom.

To be sure, girls are vulnerable to poor choices, Casanovas and creeps, unrequited love, intrigues and betrayals, and bashed reputations. As Molly Ringwald's father says in *Sixteen Candles,* "That's why they call them crushes. If they were easy, they'd call them something else."

Your daughter needs you to guide her through. Where do you start? How do you begin? Embrace an open-minded, balanced, yet watchful attitude toward your daughter's actions and reactions. Throughout the pages that come, we will guide you in creating a pattern of talking and listening that allows you to deliver what we call "romantic intelligence."

In a nutshell, cultivating romantic intelligence in your daughter is the message and the gift within the pages of this book. What do we mean exactly by romantic intelligence? Let's back up for a minute. Have your heard of the phrase "emotional intelligence"? It is a term that has been widely promoted.

Emotional intelligence means being able to recognize feelings in oneself and in others and to manage those emotions. Once children learn to identify anger, acknowledge confusion, or admit sadness, to name a few examples, they can react logically. Children with high emotional intelligence thrive.

Our concept of romantic intelligence takes a child one step further, to a place where emotions intersect with romantic attraction and actions. Romantic intelligence entails gaining insights, developing skills, seeing options, and heeding warning signs. Such knowledge will help young adolescent girls understand their feelings and desires in the arena of love. As you counsel and cultivate this romantic intelligence, your rapport becomes a process that will hardwire your child for the better. It is romantic equipment that will ensure she moves away from self-defeating romances and toward healthy relationships.

As you journey along with your child, spurred on by the information we present here, you will learn a romantic vocabulary and teach it to your daughter so she can identify her feelings and learn (and hopefully adopt) your values. In that way she creates her own ethics and standards of behavior. She will become fluent, able to express her longings and satisfaction, and cope with her losses and heartbreaks. You will be advised how to negotiate hands-on supervising and boundary setting, as well as hands-off restraint and when it's appropriate. When you know how to talk to your child, when she is alone, she will be more inclined to mull over what transpired. In private, she will weigh your words and make her own personal decisions about love and sex. You can't make those decisions for her.

With you as a confidante, she will learn to unravel some of the confusions that trip up tweenagers, and she will figure out how better to survive the loneliness, the lulls, the disappointments that scar every hopeful romantic in the game of love. And her odds for having some fun and finding true love will be enhanced.

In the chapters that follow—on the stages of love, the influence of Hollywood images, mean girls, dating, sex, and more—you will encounter a variety of issues and strategies, all of which are designed to become talking points. With your help, your daughter will have the equipment to make better decisions and bounce back from the decisions that went wrong. The intense feelings of adolescence won't be as overwhelming or as isolating for her. Nor will they be an endless source of contention between the two of you or within your family. Her crushes, jealousies, mistakes, and insecurities will become fathomable, no longer mysterious or beyond the reach of her understanding.

No one can abracadabra away teenage angst or loneliness. Nor can anyone magically program sound romantic judgment and sexual restraint. However, a parent can be instrumental. Your ears, your eyes, your shoulder, and your love are the keys. The romantic intelligence that you engender is priceless. Both you and your daughter can survive the boy-crazy times, the crushes and being crushed. The years of infatuation, melodramas, anticipation, and popularity plot lines are intense, yes, but they are intensely important, fascinating, and within your understanding. She's not out of control. Now, neither are you.

## Oops, You Did It Again: Ten Mistakes Parents Make

Surely you agree that your daughter's world is a far cry from the social scene that you knew. You need an upgrade. In order to get you started on the road to retooling your parenting skills, here is a list. By reading what others have done wrong, you can profit from their mistakes. Whether these are all new or all too familiar, don't worry. If you want to know more, rest assured. All of these talking points will be more thoroughly explored in the pages to come.

**1. Pooh-poohing intense romantic feelings.** "You're too young to feel like that!" exclaims a parent whose ten-year-old confesses she feels like dying because a boy (the one she has a crush on) refused to sit next to her on the school bus.

Puppy love is as *real* to young adolescents as it is *silly* to adults. A fifth-grader, lovesick over the class heartthrob without a chance of his returning the sentiment, or a seventh-grader devastated after a two-week tryst, appears to be acting prematurely. Despite your opinion that a sixth-grader is too young to experience valid romantic sensations (a perfectly reasonable opinion we might add), many young adolescents think love makes their roller-coaster world go round.

In a study published in *Social Psychology Quarterly*, researchers found that sixth- to eighth-grade girls assumed "one should always be in love." So don't be surprised if your child spends more time fantasizing about that boy in social studies than she spends studying for the midterm. Where will this lead? Inquiring minds at the University of Illinois discovered that teens spent more time *thinking* about the opposite sex than actually spending time with them. Yes, wanting to be attached comes with the biological clock of puberty. Intense emotions of longing, euphoria, and loss hit early and hard. Don't dismiss these feelings at the exact time when children need help getting these romantic ideas into perspective. Be gentle with tender hearts.

**2. Discounting her romantic readiness.** Okay, your daughter may not seem boy crazy. She is not "going out" with anyone. That doesn't mean she's not tuning into romantic issues or picking up relevant information. Tweenage girls dabble in romance even when they are not involved in concrete relationships themselves.

An entire fan magazine industry—*J-14, Teen Beat, Teen People*—capitalizes upon young girls' private fantasies. And almost every page features red hearts or romantic language. Those pages blow up pictorials of hotties from hit TV shows such as Jesse McCartney of *Summerland*. Remember Shaun Cassidy? Musicians from boy bands to punk poppers delight avid readers. Think Maroon 5. Think back to the Backstreet Boys and all the way to the Beatles. Actors are always posing and there's always someone new and hot. Do you know who the "it" star is now? Girls devour these magazines, peruse the pinups, and cover their walls with pix of their idols, and in so doing, explore the terrain of infatuation and even (ouch) lust.

The girl with no real boys in her personal life is nevertheless impressionable. In all likelihood she is secretly pining. Many become sounding boards for those who are in the throes of romance. Conversations introduce even the most disinterested and innocent or shy to scenarios and scripts about making out and breaking up. In this third-person way, girls learn about peer mores and ethics, about cultural customs and messages.

Staying in touch with a girl means being involved *before* you think you need to be.

**3. Overinvesting in her romance.** Over our years of being a shoulder online and off for worried parents of tweens and teens, we have heard repeatedly, "I hate my daughter's boyfriend." When so many other parents hate the boys upon whom their daughters fixate, you feel lucky because you absolutely love your daughter's new boyfriend. This is how the mother who opened her wallet and took out the photograph of her fourteen-year-old daughter's boyfriend felt. She showed off his picture and sang his praises as if she were a new parent bragging over a shot of her newborn. This mother even went so far as to admit, "He is perfect and I'd be happy if my daughter married him—someday." You could almost see this balloon sprout over her head: a wedding scene, the bride blushing and her mother teary-eyed.

No matter how much you love your daughter's choice in middle school, hold off your endorsement. The same goes for playing matchmaker with a shy daughter and a boy you think would be great for her. He may be cute, smart, a great athlete, from a good family, a gentleman, and more—but this is way too soon for you to weigh in by reinforcing a romance or ramming one down your daughter's throat.

Young adolescents are prone to rushing into romance all on their own. Your encouragement could intensify their penchant. If your child is not rushing, respect her timing. Resist the urge to include "him" on family outings or at holiday dinners as if he's part of the family. We've heard of parents nonchalantly saying it's fine if a boyfriend sleeps over—on the family couch. In the early adolescent years, girls need you to put the brakes on their romantic passions. They need you to help them evaluate the good and the bad aspects of a boy, a crush, a relationship—not to vote yea or nay.

If you favor a boy too earnestly, your daughter may feel reluctant to move on and may ignore her own inner voice. Or she may ditch him because she doesn't want your unabashed approval. Rebellious streaks can rear their prickly heads here. Likewise, keep feelings of dislike to a minimum, unless he's really bad news.

Keep in mind that these are not the years to expect anything to last.

**4. Flirting with her beau.** Don't act like one of those desperate housewives on Wisteria Lane. Middle age can make a woman feel unattractive. Seeking attention and reassurance that you are still sexy is understandable and acceptable, so long as you don't use a daughter's date or boyfriend for that reassurance. And don't try to get friendly with a boy that your daughter thinks is hot and would like to get to know better.

You'll know when you have committed such sins because your daughter will be furious with you. Or her face will color with embarrassment. Chances are that she will comment that you were too friendly, acting ridiculous, or lame. Rather than getting defensive or even trying to explain, just honor her discomfort. Promise that you will cultivate more reserve, and butt out in the future.

**5. Giving mixed messages.** Mothers and fathers are often on different pages in the family guidebook of love. Is one of you strict and overprotective while the other tends to be permissive? Are you reasonable while your spouse isn't? As one fifteen-year-old quipped, "My dad is not someone to talk to at all. He's one of those who wants to get out the machete every time a boy walks through the door."

Compare and contrast how you both react to boys, and to

curfews and what happens when they are broken. Discuss and agree on dating rules and whether or not your daughter should be allowed to entertain a boy in her bedroom. Having and sending contradictory messages sabotages your daughter and your intended family values. Get on the same page, even when it entails compromise.

**6. Third-degreeing after a social event or date.** Asking rhetorically, "Did you have a nice time?" is not the same thing as the Inquisition. Many of the girls we interviewed bristled about returning home only to undergo sessions that made them feel as if they were in the police station under suspicion for a crime. For instance, the mother of a tween on the shy side might bombard her with twenty questions about the school dance such as:

- Did anyone ask you to dance?
- Did the boys congregate on one side and the girls on the other?
- Was there a Sadie Hawkins or Ladies' Choice moment?
- Did you tap anyone's shoulder when the DJ played a slow song?

A father worried about his precocious child might batter her with

- How much dirty dancing went down?
- Did you spend the whole night glued to that new friend of yours?

The following came courtesy of a sixteen-year-old girl and her take on the appropriate timing and pace of talk: "When a girl comes home after a dance, a party or a date all glowing and happy, don't ruin her mood with twenty-one questions! Girls like me want some time to ourselves, to bask in that moment of happiness."

The reverse holds true as well. She added, "If she comes

home crying and heads to her room, don't barge in. Knock. Wait. Ask if you can help."

By giving your daughter space, you allow her to process her euphoria or her pain in the privacy of her own thoughts. Afterward, she will be better able to explain how she feels and admit your input. You should let her know that you are there to share the romantic high points and the social disappointments and gaffes. You shouldn't rush in immediately.

**7. Pressuring her friends or her boyfriend for inside information about her love life.** Ten- to fifteen-year-olds crave a private life. This development is natural. In order to maintain a sense of privacy, they can become secretive. Your daughter may deliberately withhold the exact social details, those same details that you feel obligated to uncover as a responsible parent.

You ask, "Is this boy, Joshua, more than a friend?"

She says, "I don't know" dismissively.

You may be dying to know more, but she stonewalls you. Don't go outside and pry into her affairs by pinning down her friends. Interrogating her peers may seem more urgent if you get wind of a rumor swirling around your daughter. You hear that her circle of friends got drunk or that she was spotted hanging out on a street corner with a notorious so-and-so over the weekend (when she told you she went to a sleepover).

Yes, it is your duty as a concerned parent to investigate any rumor. However, the best way to start is by sharing the gossip directly with your child. Give her the opportunity to clarify, refute, or explain herself. Checking facts behind her back is guaranteed to ruin the trust that you need to build with her at this point in her life.

**8. Letting your past haunt her present.** When you were in junior high (that's what middle school was called back then) or high school, were you popular—well liked, with many friends, and included in social events? Over our years of discussing the pros and cons of being popular with many, many mothers of young adolescent girls, we have often heard them refer to their status. Some were hip, the translation for today's hot. Others confessed to being incredibly lonely, perennial wallflowers.

Mothers who felt popular wanted their daughters to be likewise and to share in the heady, exciting social whirl. Mothers whose memory stung with pain because they felt unpopular—meaning they didn't have many friends and weren't privy to parties and prestigious social standing—wanted their daughters to avoid this left-out fate. Both tended to put pressure on their girls to go for the brass ring of popularity. Not a few offered advice such as what clothes to wear or how she should fix her hair. Some concocted schemes to advance a daughter's popularity. "I started a mother-daughter book club and invited those top-rung girls that ordinarily were out of reach," offered a mother whose plan to get her child into the in-crowd worked.

It's natural for you to want the best for your children. Friends, frequent invitations, and fun sound like the right social recipe. *Stop yourself.* This is not your life or a second chance for you to vicariously redo your life. Your daughter is a different entity with a different personality and unique goals. Give her the freedom to live out her own story whether she's destined for a popular ride or not. Don't rush her. For example, if a big social event lies on the horizon and she wants to go as part of a group, don't suggest she ask a date.

If you need further convincing, consider this. In this day and age, popularity isn't simple. The popular crowd faces temptations (experimentation with alcohol, drugs, and sexual activity) that can cancel out any benefits.

Don't fail to see that middle school and high school are complex social systems. There is vast territory in between being an "it" girl and an outcast. A girl can have a few good friends and attend a party here and there, enjoy being a teenager without being in the in crowd or being the object of their scorn. Look for her comfort level, not yours.

**9. Levying sexist, unequal dating rules.** Do you pay closer attention to the social comings and goings of your daughter(s) compared to your son(s)? If you give more leeway to boys, and set more lenient rules for them, you are like many parents. Harris Interactive Youth Query, an online poll, in 2003 asked teen boys and girls ages eight to eighteen about the boundaries imposed by parents surrounding dating. In all responses to queries about time curfews, going out during the week, social destination, and general rules, girls had *higher* percentages of supervision and *less* freedom. When you have a double standard regarding romantic freedom, you send a message that your daughter needs more protection. You imply she may have less sense and be less able to take care of herself.

*Both* boys and girls need guidance and empowerment. Each child, regardless of gender, needs guidance about things like safety, stalkers, and safe sex. Both genders benefit from having enough rope to swing to new heights romantically or to hang themselves. (We spend an entire chapter priming you for the sex education tenets that your child needs from you.) In the scope of the tween years, mistakes and mishaps provide experiences for learning and growing.

**10. Letting your window of opportunity shut.** Kids on the cusp of early adolescence (eight to twelve-year-olds) credit mom (68 percent) or dad (47 percent) with teaching them about love and relationships. Then thirteen arrives. At that chronological turning point, only 33 percent of kids (thirteen to eighteen) look to mom and only 15 percent look to dad. Note that the window of opportunity for inculcating your family and romantic values gradually closes as children move through their teens. That means it is brief.

Are you guilty of these mistakes? If you are feeling anxious again, disheartened, overwhelmed, take heart. By the time you reach our last page, you will have a different perspective on the romantic life of the young. Not only will you be in a better mood for love pertaining to your tween, but you will be more qualified to be the romantic mentor and manager that your daughter needs. Take a few words of wisdom from the Wizard of Oz who said, "Hearts will never be practical until they are made unbreakable."

You cannot make over your little girl's heart into an unbreakable model, but we promise that you can give her practical help and, yes, even some wisdom.

# CHAPTER 2

# Girl, You'll Be a Woman Soon

## *The Ages and Stages That Govern Love*

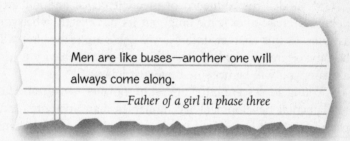

> Men are like buses—another one will always come along.
>
> —*Father of a girl in phase three*

Have you ever noticed one of the first things nearly all girls do at the start of early adolescence? They let their hair grow longer. Hours evaporate in the care of hair: shampooing, conditioning, blow-drying, highlighting, color-streaking, curling, straightening, thickening, braiding, beading, dreadlocking, cornrowing, crimping.

It's as if they've gone up into the attic of childhood and dusted off that tale of Rapunzel. Girls head toward their bedroom whenever they feel a parent's disapproval. It can feel like a lonely tower. These little princesses spin fantasies about handsome princes. Longer hair feels right. Mythically and methodically, girls grow those tresses, coiffing themselves for escape from the confines of King Daddy to fairy-tale happily-ever-after endings.

Like coveting long hair, much of a girl's romantic awakening is instinctive, too.

You may be thinking: I already know that. Everyone gets the connection that raging hormones propel girls toward love. We tend to think of girls in early adolescence as getting boy crazy overnight, preoccupied and totally obsessed. Many mothers have used expressions like "a switch flipped," as in one day she was my little girl and at the flip of a switch she changed. Truth be told, though, a young adolescent's social coming of age happens in layers.

Girls under the influence of preadolescence and puberty definitely chase after something, but it's not exactly what you assume. As this chapter unfolds, what girls are really after will become clearer. If you hope that this boy-crazy behavior is just a phase, you will be reassured by what follows.

A young adolescent girl's interest in romance is natural. This fundamental development fact unnerves many parents. As a parent, you will be relieved to know that on the inside tweens proceed in stages. Social and romantic behaviors truly follow a pattern of phases. If you've never heard this before, that's because research tends toward the negative. Rather than teach us how to understand the young, it tries to show us how to "fix" them. Rarely do social scientists delve into the behavior of ordinary teenagers. The details of perfectly normal emerging sexuality get short shrift, according to scholar B. Bradford Brown. Remarking on this shortcoming in *The Development of Romantic Relationships in Adolescence,* she says, "Adolescents may belabor the intricacies of teenage romance hour after hour in songs on the radio or shows on television, but most adult researchers seem to be tuned to a different channel. It is high time [to] dive into this intense, emotional, and fascinating aspect of the adolescent experience."

And so we will. We will explain the ages and stages of romantic thinking and actions, what really happens underneath the surface of giggling, lovesick ordinary tweens. A girl's forwardness, her jealousies, her dreaming, scheming, and mooning over boys have a pattern. Rather than spending your time and energy trying to turn back the pubescent biological clock, an enlightened and better strategy will be to digest the changes. Grasping each of the stages one by one will provide you with a useful perspective. Once you have this framework, you will become better equipped as the romantically savvy mentor, the sage with good advice that your little girl needs.

According to Brown's research, preadolescent girl crushes and romantic dramas actually unfold in a sequence of four phases. Within each phase, girls are driven by typical motives. They hold and harbor specific intentions. Their behavior is geared toward a target audience. Learning what occurs in the course of each phase enables you to monitor your daughter's romantic readiness and growth. Furthermore, you then can help her process this precious time and part of her life as a young woman.

## The Phases of a Girl's Mooning

### Phase One: From Cooties to Cuties

> *Circle, circle, dot, dot,*
> *Now I have my cootie shot.*
> *Circle, circle, square, square,*
> *Now I have it everywhere.*

After pre-K and prior to early adolescence, children prefer the company of their own gender. Girls stick with girls; boys stick with boys. Genders are apt to squeal about "cooties" when the opposite sex enters the picture. Then a shift takes place. Young adolescents are no longer content with same-sex company. Mixed company becomes compelling. Usually, girls' flirting radar engages first. This change of heart can hit a girl at ten, even eight, or not happen until she's older.

This happens partly because of biology, as puberty engineers the attraction, but not entirely. Peers can push one another into socializing with the opposite sex. Even a girl who has not entered puberty can become immersed in boy-crazy scheming because her girlfriends are. She may not personally feel the pull toward boys because her hormones have not ignited yet, but she does understand the pull of wanting to fit in with whatever the group does.

Phase one serves as a girl's *initiation* into the game of love. Think of this step as a kind of announcement, her social coming-out party. With the onset of this phase, a girl's identity embraces a new characteristic—feeling and acting romantic.

Ten- to fifteen-year-olds wrestle with questions about identity. *Who am I? Am I lovable?* As much as parents would love to be able to answer these questions for their children, they cannot. At least not in a way that will satisfy their daughter. The answers to such pivotal, psychic queries about personality, worth, and lovability come from other children. As they put together the pieces to their personal puzzles, girls and boys compare and contrast themselves to one another. They begin to develop an image of their romantic selves.

Socializing resembles a performance and becomes paramount to their quest. Consider this vignette.

Mrs. Jones, Cynthia's mom, drives the car pool for her daughter's dance class. Making casual conversation, she asks the girls in the backseat,

"What's new in school?"

"This afternoon at recess Mark and I got married on the playground," ten-year-old Carrie giggles.

Each of the backseat brigade interrupts with details.

"I married them," Lizzie offered, repeating, "Mark, do you take Carrie for your bride for better or for worse." Bursts of laughter erupt in the rear.

Jennifer says, "I was the ring bearer because I had a ring pop in my backpack." Carrie pushes her ring-popped finger into Mrs. Jones's cheek.

"We all cried because . . ." one of them begins, but then all in unison sigh, "Carrie and Mark make such a cute couple."

If you hear strands of "Going to the Chapel" and feel like telephoning the mother of the bride, hold off. Let's take a minute to put the wedding into a developmental perspective.

What message does the bride intend to broadcast? Carrie loves Mark, right? No. The tableau isn't about Mark at all. The boy is little more than a foil. Carrie created her drama to make a statement. "I am a romantic now" she says of her evolution. She adds this characteristic to her portfolio of other personal details that include being athletic, smart, energetic. The playground nuptials are symbolic, meant to convey that Carrie has boarded the love boat. It's all about her.

Who is the target for Carrie's announcement? Mark? Nope. The message, first and foremost, is Carrie's. She's getting her feet wet in the sensations of feeling attracted to boys. Carrie allows a new layer of her personality to emerge, her romantic self. That said and done, her target audience expands to include her girlfriends, other peers, and the rest of her world.

Critical to understanding each phase is identifying a child's intention. What is Carrie's intention? Is it to commit and pledge her love to Mark? Not at all. Carrie's desire revolves around exploring this new romantic dimension, to bask in its thrill, and to come to know how it feels to be a girl in love. She's trying it on for size. This tableau has little to do with the boy. It's more Carrie's personal affair, and Mark will be history in weeks, or days, most likely even hours.

In this case, the wedding felt highly satisfying because it accomplished Carrie's goal. She becomes the center of attention, showing the world that she is ready, willing, and able to express romantic feelings.

Keep in mind that not all girls are as forward as Carrie. Others may announce their romantic selves in different ways. A girl's notebook may be covered with the fantasy signature doodling of Mrs. Brad Pitt. Or her closet may start to fill up with clothing more suited to dating than dressing like a little girl. For young adolescent girls, most first romantic crushes and chases are designed to signal a turning point in the way a girl sees herself.

## Phase Two: When He's Hot, She's Cool

Throughout early adolescence, children try to fit in. All desperately long to be accepted by their peers. Our first book, *The Roller-Coaster Years: Raising Your Child Through the Maddening Yet Magical Middle School Years,* charted the typical fears of ten- to fifteen-year-olds. Social anxiety, worry about what friends think about them, ranks first on the worry meter according to young adolescents. Polling middle school teachers added credence as they agreed that fretting about friends topped the fear list for kids.

That explains why, for young adolescents, popularity becomes the ideal. It is a goal, the stuff of fantasy, and the dream of nearly all, whether or not they have the potential to be class president, the top jock, or the prom queen. School popularity is the tweenage definition of celebrity.

Phase two of this development takes hold when a girl uses romance for popularity. She makes the connection that being linked romantically earns her social status or sets her back. Remember Carrie and her mock wedding? That setup basically was a one-woman drama. Now the romantic plots twist and turn on the social effect a crush generates.

To illustrate this phase, meet eighth-grader Stephanie. Stephanie's mother told us, "In the last few weeks my thirteen-year-old's look has gone from childish to sexy." To paraphrase her, Stef is a beauty with beautiful caramel-hued Caribbean skin. Her older sister taught her how to apply makeup to make her lips shine and her cheeks glow. Curves have been pushing outward. Stef emphasizes these with snug white T-shirts and jeans tightly hugging newly forming hips. Stef, the other girls say, looks like Ashanti, the famous hip-hop star.

Stef recently made the cheerleading squad. The middle

school squad attended the high school football game to watch the older girls' cheer routines. Lamar, the varsity football team's best player, flirted with Stef. He's seventeen. Overnight, Stef and Lamar are the lead in the middle school gossip mill. Rumor has it that Lamar will ask Stef out. With her potential new beau, Stephanie's popularity skyrockets.

While other girls (and a few mothers) envy Stephanie's rising social star, her own mother feels scared. To her way of thinking, for a thirteen-year-old innocent, Lamar spells trouble.

Acknowledging and analyzing the young cheerleader's enviable position with a phase two approach can ground both mother and daughter. What is the message that Stephanie wants to communicate? Could it be that the eighth-grader believes that she is ready to date older boys? That's jumping the gun, really. Plain and simple, Stef loves the attention mainly because Lamar's interest in her confers prestige. With every gossip tidbit, Stephanie edges higher and higher up the eighth-grade food chain of who's who.

Who's Stephanie trying to impress? In other words, who is the target for this message? Lamar? Does she want Lamar to know how eager she is to get to know him? Not primarily, if at all. It's her girlfriends, Nicole and Jenna, and maybe that Christina (who thinks she's all that) that probably matter most. The *I'm-cool-because-an-older-boy-wants-me* compliment is aimed at her peers.

What does Stephanie want? What's her intention? To further enchant and intrigue Lamar? A young adolescent in phase two does not have the maturity yet to focus on the boy. She is still self-absorbed. Her crush qualifies as a social affair, not an interpersonal event between a boy and a girl. The emphasis lies *not* on the boy (similar to phase one) or on structuring a meaningful relationship with him. In this phase romantic motives are inextricably linked to other people's reaction. It's all about improving social status.

Not every girl will sweep a football star off his feet. Many more will moon over the older or most popular boy in school. Just zeroing in on a hot hunk, talking about him all the time, and plotting to bump into him can enhance a girl's esteem in the eyes of her less daring peers.

You may be thinking that all this analysis is useless. The real point comes once parents like Stephanie's have to decide: Is their daughter old enough to date? Even a phantom choice, a boy she is only daydreaming about, can scare a parent. Countless girls want to date before their parents think it appropriate.

How does a parent discourage a girl from falling for an older boy or for a boy who clearly constitutes a poor choice? Talking with a girl about what she really wants and helping her see her true motives is never a waste of time. In this case, Stephanie, at thirteen, may be so busy bathing in the prestige that dating a high school junior brings that she fails to recognize the danger. A parent needs to make her aware of the possibilities. Socializing with Lamar brings tricky baggage. An older crowd, a popular bunch, inevitably will tempt a girl with risky situations— unchaperoned parties, underage drinking, smoking marijuana, expectations about sexual activity.

Younger girls who long to socialize with older teens or hang out with their older sibling's pals need to be prepared for feelings that are bound to surface in such scenarios. Namely that they may want to act older and, therefore, feel pressured to drink, smoke, or have sex. Tweenagers loathe feeling like babies, especially in the company of older adolescents.

## Phase Three: Just the Two of Us

Generally speaking, girls will stay absorbed in the first two phases of romantic behavior between the ages of ten and fifteen. Because puberty strikes different girls at different times, it is impossible to erect strict age classifications. Suffice it to say that forming a new, womanly self-image, taking the temperature of a fluctuating popularity, and wrestling with fragile self-esteem is a full-time job for tweenagers.

With later adolescence, though, comes a deeper understanding of romantic notions. As a girl moves through the teen years she comes to feel more comfortable with her romantic dimension. She outgrows the mentality that evaluates every action and decision in terms of how her friends react. At this juncture, a girl envisions the mutual romantic feelings involved in a budding relationship. By phase three a girl can actually see the boy for who he is as a person. He no longer chiefly serves as a prop or a tool to higher status, or conversely, a trap to lower status.

Phase three features the capacity for mutual affection. Some girls find a boy and experience a two-way romance. Others develop that capacity for mutual love but don't find that special someone. Dealing with loneliness and longing or unrequited love takes center stage. Yes, girls now enter complicated waters.

Sixteen-year-old Andrea shows the transition. Before falling for David, Andrea spent every weekend at her best friend's house or else her best friend slept over at Andrea's, according to her mother. Now, Andrea's mom nostalgically admits, "I used to hate those sleepovers. The girls kept me up half the night. The next day Andrea and I acted cranky and fought all through the day. Now I long for those sleep-deprived days."

Why the turnaround? Since Andrea met boyfriend, David, every weekend the two snuggle on her family couch or his, watching movies or playing video games. Then there are the parties.

"I worry," says the sixteen-year-old's mom, "about Andrea doing things she'll regret."

What message comes from Andrea now? Andrea loves David? Now, the answer is yes. She wants to build a relationship with him, not only for herself personally, but for the sake of her feelings for him as an individual too. Furthermore, she wants to experience being part of a couple. What does togetherness feel like? What do couples talk about? Older adolescents become engaged with these romantic explorations.

Is Andrea showing off by having a steady boyfriend for the

## THE SECRET DISCIPLINE WEAPON

Nearly every decision a young adolescent makes about her peers or close friends, boys, or her social life can be distilled into two words: *cool* and *fool*. Think about it. That fashion look she's trying for, the impression she hopes to make—most girls say they just want to be perceived as cool. The ultimate dread is to appear foolish, or uncool.

Use this cool-fool dichotomy and dynamic to your advantage. Frame your discipline tactics and set your limits by using the *cool/fool* words. For example:

**Your daughter wants to go to a party that will be attended by older teens or a fast crowd.**

**DON'T SAY:** No, because I said so.

**DO SAY:** I don't think that's a good idea because these older or wilder kids may pressure you. They might be doing things that will make you feel uncomfortable. You may be put in a predicament: do something you know is wrong or look like a fool. They may even take pleasure in making you into a fool so they can look cooler—meaner but cooler.

**Your daughter picks out a tight white dress that is clingy, clearly too sexy in your view.**

**DON'T SAY:** You look too sexy.

**DO SAY:** White is a very tricky color. Your panty lines, the wrong light, feeling chilled or hot—you could wind up showing more than you want to, looking foolish.

**Your daughter is infatuated with a wild boy, a delin-
quent to your way of thinking.**

DON'T SAY: Paul is too wild. He's a loser.
DO SAY: Paul's wild ways seem cool, but wait. Suppose
   he gets arrested for drunk driving. That's not cool.

Use your imagination. You can spin nearly every
dilemma into the cool/fool conversation. Rather than appearing authoritarian, you appear socially savvy. You can
draw her into discussion about all sorts of possibilities
that may arise. This think-ahead and plan-ahead scenario
is a great exercise and a wonderful precedent.

Your child will respond far more positively to what you
are saying when you frame rules around how certain behaviors could affect her social image. The thought of stepping into embarrassing no-win situations or into mean
gossip and scandal that could ruin her reputation will
give a girl pause.

No discipline tactic is guaranteed, but this one will be
far more effective than just saying no. You are manipulat-
ing her insecurities, yes. But sometimes the end justifies
the means.

benefit of her friends? No. What her girlfriends say about
David or think about the couple, the importance of such reviews mostly drop off the radar of older teenagers.

In fact, it's typical for a girl with a boyfriend to drop her
friends at this phase, especially if her girlfriends don't have special someones. When and if a girl does treat her girlfriends like

second fiddles, bad feelings and even fights can erupt among them.

What are Andrea's intentions? Expressing intimacy, definitely. How? The words "I like you a lot" and "I love you" are spoken. Her actions are likely to include sexual intimacy from kissing to other forms of sexual experimentation. Gifts and love notes are exchanged. By inviting her boyfriend to family events, she mimics what couples do in mature relationships.

The romantic agenda of older teenagers consists of physical and emotional discoveries, the meat and potatoes of relationships. Getting to know a boy as a person and a nurturing partner is of primary importance. Is he trustworthy, tender, and caring? Can they share secrets? Do they enjoy mutual interests? This phase also entails learning much about managing a relationship. Empathy. Sacrifice. Equality. Patience. These partnership issues come into play.

A girl without a boyfriend is likely to mope around because she is missing out on all this. Or she may be feeling left behind because her best friends have deserted her for love. Managing conflict and emotions comes into play here for both those who have a boyfriend and those who don't. Desire and values clash for those in love. Desire and reality clash for those longing for love.

Deep romantic waters signal danger. How much sexual experimentation and intimacy adolescent girls engage in depends on many things. For example, what values have you engendered? Have you talked about when sexual activity is appropriate? What supervision and rules have you set? Watching over the young lovers counts, even though you have lost the ability to monitor your daughter every waking hour of the day. In the end, the extent to which a daughter has embraced your values and rules determines her course of erotic action.

Be firm with a young girl in love. Be gentle with a girl who has an achy-breaky heart, who longs for love she has not found.

## Phase Four: Bonding for the Future

In later adolescence, girls graduate to evaluating boys as potential long-term partners. The concept of the future surfaces in a girl's mind. This occurs when girls are dating for real or even when they are focusing on would-be suitors. Compatibility becomes a priority along with other qualifiers.

A young woman begins to visualize where she wants to go after high school. She contemplates decisions: Will she or won't she move on to college? Or a vocational program? Or a full-time job? Is marriage a goal on the immediate agenda or does she want to focus on professional goals first and marriage and children later? When it comes to a mate now, a girl's evaluations turn pragmatic. Does a romantic partner fit into her life plan and her love plan? Can he commit? Is he capable of compromise on issues that are important to her? What about his work-related aspirations and ambitions? Is this person an acceptable mate? Does he want the same things in life that she deems important? Money, status, family, geography—the considerations multiply. The goal for a girl in this phase climaxes with every new romantic coupling: Does this person measure up as a life companion, or not?

In the focus groups we met with across the country while preparing for this book, girls confided generously. In a suburb outside of Washington, DC, a vivacious dark-haired high school senior volunteered that she'd been compiling a boyfriend wish list since middle school. Everyone in our focus group begged to see it. Graciously, she scrambled back to her locker and returned with this:

**What I Look for in a Boy**
Over 5´9˝
good hair
nice eyes, nice hip bones, nice stomach
funny
no mustache thing

no big nose
   dresses well
   doesn't scratch himself in public
   nice smile, twinkly
   compliments me
   likes to go out
   has nice friends
      tells me what he's feeling
      not two-faced
      loves talking to me
      supports me
      good kisser
         likes kids
         has some money
         has nice parents
         doesn't have a problem with me hanging out with
           other people
         will travel the world with me

Look closely, and what becomes apparent is the progression of her requirements. You can almost see her advancing through the phases. In the beginning, it's all about what turns her on to a boy and what physical cues rev her romantic engine. Good hair and taut stomach are a plus, but not facial hair. Those phase two "what-will-my-tweenage-friends-think" calculations rear their head next as she ticks off social assets and liabilities of his that will reflect upon her status. Clearly a boy's clothes, connections, and affectations will make or break the love match. Then the adolescent coupling urge dominates as the caveats turn to items synonymous with trust ("not two-faced") and intimacy ("loves talking to me" as well as "good kisser"). And finally, you can see the bonding computations as she factors in a boy's take on kids, his earning power, and whether or not he meets her life-size and lifelong expectations.

Within her laundry list are the four phases: identity (I am interested in love); status (the right boy can help me fit in); affection (the give and take of intimacy); bonding (thinking about a romantic partnership for life). That summarizes the overview that every parent needs to comprehend as a backdrop.

## The Phantom Crush . . .
## Tears on My Pillow

Behavioral experts point out that young and older adolescents might not march handily from one phase to the next in exact progression. In our explanation of the phases, we used examples of girls already involved with boys. Yet a whole legion of shy and awkward girls exists, made up of girls who aren't hooking up innocently on the playground or rushing off to parties. Nor do all girls easily find the boyfriend they want when they want him. Some girls never get a chance to have their hearts broken. Just ask songwriters, the one who penned "Dream Lover" or "Hey Venus." While parents may be thrilled not to have to wonder if a child is having sex with her boyfriend, they should know that their child is probably wishing that she had someone to whom she could say no.

Like the imaginary friend invented to play with a lonely young child, tweenagers often construct phantom crushes to love. At thirteen or fourteen, many girls fall hard for a sports icon or a teen idol. She may ask you to pay for the Sports Channel on cable so she can watch hockey hunks slice the ice. A girl may memorize a songwriter's lyrics as if the brooding bard meant every word as a personal poem just for her. Hours are spent on the Internet scouring for all the personal details about the life of her crush. To a young heart, these make-believe romances seem absolutely real. When in his "Dancing in the Dark" video Bruce Springsteen pulls a girl (the unknown Courtney Cox) out of a crowd of fans and up onto the stage, the video is depicting the fantasy of countless girls.

It's not unusual for a pack of friends to share a crush. In Judy Blume's classic novel *Are You There God? It's Me, Margaret,* all four pals list Philip Leroy (the best-looking boy in class) as their top choice. Other girls keep their fantasy man a secret. Some may resort to pretending they have a secret admirer. Remember poor Jan Brady on *The Brady Bunch* faking a telephone call from George, umm, Glass, asking her for a date?

The rule here is to be gentle with their fragile hearts and phantom loves. Don't tell your tween that buying a teddy bear to toss up on stage during a concert is wasting her birthday money. Don't let siblings make fun of sisters who hide secret crushes. Realize that phantom crushes have an important role to play: They make love democratic, available for everyone. They enable the shy and the awkward to ease into those universal feelings of longing and anticipation, and at times even bliss. Yes, when Jesse McCartney sings about loving a girl's beautiful soul, a girl can feel he is singing to her. It's just a matter of time before the phantom crush will be left behind, put onto the proverbial shelf next to where imaginary friends dwell.

As with all changes, whether physical or emotional, during these years children mature at different paces to the tune of an individual timetable. However, having a developmental map provides you with an invaluable guide. With more knowledge and compassion you can watch a girl get ready, get set, and go on to the game of love.

## What a Girl Wants, What a Girl Needs

As a girl moves through the ages and stages of romance, psychology and sociology and physiology all affect her. Chemistry percolates in the air. If your child's socializing is beginning to sound like a university curriculum, don't worry. In a way that's exactly what it is.

What does your daughter want in phase one? Two? Three? Four? If the answer that keeps popping into your mind is always the same—a boyfriend—realize that a girl's needs are deeper than what is obvious. She doesn't always realize what she wants exactly or how her "wants" differ from what she needs. It's your job to help her clarify things, to keep her safe, and help her grow into a caring individual.

So, phase by phase, here are some strategic guidelines, even though the same issues may surface over again in more than one phase.

### Phase One

When a girl wants everyone to notice her new romantic self, signals start. One may be exhibiting a more grown-up fashion style. When she shops, her choices are more stylish and sexy, maybe too much so. She may begin wearing makeup or pestering you to let her. She chooses friends who are inclined to do as she is doing. She wants boys to notice her and maybe even ask her to "go out with" them (meaning meeting at lockers in school and walking from class to class holding hands). She wants opportunities for a coming-out party.

What a girl needs is for you to recognize her evolution and to validate it, not necessarily to green-light every one of her plans. The first time your ten- or eleven-year-old talks about buying a bra, or wears one, or when she looks at a skimpy out-fit in a store, watch your reactions. Don't tease her. Make sure your husband and your daughter's siblings don't either. Think back to how you felt when you got teased about budding breasts. Do say, "You are looking grown up these days." Let her know that others are noticing, her, too. If you don't like her dark lipstick or a fashion buy, gently suggest that waiting until next year would be better for that selection. Don't say, "Take those tight pants back. You are not going out looking like that!" At this point, a girl needs your recognition of her growing up. It's all right for her to want to attract attention to that fact. However, let her know that is not the same thing as your per-mission to let her grow up too fast.

## Phase Two

What a girl wants is free rein to work her odds at the popularity jackpot. That can mean endless cell phoning and IMing wherein a great deal of spats unravel—who likes whom and who said what and how this ruined so-and-so's reputation. Fights and hurt feelings and confusing explanations are typical. She'll push your limits and ethics trying to make social points or not lose them. She will be very sensitive to peer opinion and pressure. Expect her to argue, "Everyone else is allowed."

What a girl needs here is to learn how to balance her individuality with her desire to belong. For instance, if she wants to drop her old best friend, ask her why? Okay, so what if Bethany still acts like a baby, is that a reason to hurt her? Ask: Is a good person like Bethany worth less or is she less deserving than a cool person? Nudge your daughter to weigh the consequences of her decisions. Guide her to define her individual self and to nourish that part of her. See that she understands the concepts of right and wrong in the midst of desperately trying to fit in. When you say no, give her a good reason, not "Because I said so." When you give the reasons behind your decisions, you help her look at the reasons behind hers.

## Phase Three

A girl wants a private life in which to exercise her capacity for mutual affection. She will have secrets and divulge confessions to her friends. She will have risky ideas and have to decide whether or not to act on them. She will be weighing emotional high and low points. She may want to keep you out of her most private thoughts and actions. This stage is harder for her and for you as sexual activity may start.

What a girl needs is for you to acknowledge and respect her privacy. Be direct if you have a concern. If you aren't, you will lose credibility. As one girl explained, "My mother says, 'Oh did you have fun?' Or 'How was the party?' Her tone gives her away. What she really means is 'Did you drink?' When she asks me, 'Did you like the movie?' what she really means is 'Did you watch the movie?' She's implying I might have spent the whole time making out. Or she wants a movie review to make sure that's really where I went."

Don't snoop to uncover every detail of her relationship with a new boy. Don't pry or push to stay on top of her every social mistake or failure. Let her take the initiative. On the other hand, be firm about family rules. If she breaks the rules, enforce consequences. Supervise.

### Phase Four

A girl wants everlasting love from a boy and from you. On the road to this blissful, wistful goal, there are many bumps, bruises, creeps, and pitfalls. She may not share all of it with you. That's okay.

"We girls learn from interacting with each other and with boys," insists a sixteen-year-old. And her classmate jumps in with, "Yeah and we learn best from fumbling through our mistakes."

What a girl needs is to feel your love and your willingness to assist her in getting the love she wants. Give her space while at the same time communicating how she can proceed in healthy and safe ways. She needs your approval and guidance through the ups and downs, the pleasures and mistakes implicit in romantic relationships.

## Fathers (and Mothers), Be Good to Your Daughters

Along the way, snags and snits are inevitable. Reduce hard feelings with these three tactics.

**Don't be overly negative.** Admittedly, this is easier to do in the first two phases before images of your daughter having sex loom in your mind. Girls are very perceptive. They interpret negativity as disapproval. When we asked girls, What kinds of conversations do you have with your parents about your social life? it was clear from their answers that they picked up bad vibes right away.

"I'd have to say that my conversations come down to what I call alarmist talk. My mother doesn't say it, but she expects the worst," offered a thirteen-year-old.

When your demeanor belies a steady stream of distrust or distress about your child's every social move, you and she are on a collision course. Her natural urges to socialize and explore intimacy coupled with your determination to nip it in the bud destine your relationship to resemble two locomotives speeding toward a train wreck. Her social life turns into the control issue in your household. You say no too often. She tears up to her bedroom and slams the door behind her. And then she shuts you—along with your advice—out. You do not want to be the last person she comes to with a question, a worry, or a problem.

**Don't jump to conclusions; help your daughter come to her own conclusions.** Acknowledging that a girl is not terminally boy crazed at eleven, twelve, or thirteen gives you permission to feel relief. You can concentrate on your role to guide her toward understanding the stirrings of love and help her get her needs met. Or help her cope. Ask her about and discuss her motives and intentions. See if she can answer the question: Who am I trying to please and why? You can't engage in these kinds of valuable Q&A sessions when your sole agenda revolves around squelching ardent feelings or young love.

When you are positive and open-minded your rapport will flourish. Take this remark, "My mom's curious. I like that. She's really willing to listen to me instead of jumping in with advice before I even finish one sentence," admitted a thirteen-year-old.

And a sixteen-year-old added, "I can listen to my dad because he was a guy. You know what I mean. He's still a guy of course. But he was the age of my boyfriend once. He knows how boys think. He tries to explain things to me."

Given a choice between talking to the Terminator or to a more reasonable parent, whom will a girl choose? The answer, of course, is a calm, approachable parent.

**Do keep the line clear between being her parent and being her friend.** This can be a challenge during any phase and throughout your child's life. Think of your child's romantic fixation like this: if you can't beat her; join her. Become one with her interest in boys, without being too permissive, of course. As you build good camaraderie by listening to what Brittany did to Bobby and how Jennifer cried over not being invited to Sally's party, don't forget you are the adult. It's easy to get sucked into girls' feuds, which always have some tie to a boy. It's her soap opera, not yours. Your part is to help her deal, not jump into the fray. Rather than micromanage her social rise, fix her failures or fallouts, or call another mother to make suggestions, give her room to try her own solutions.

A final thought: keep your eye on the long-term goal—helping your daughter manage romantic longing, solve popularity puzzles, and navigate dating games. You want to help her lay a firm foundation of herself as an individual and as a loving and lovable young woman.

# CHAPTER 3

# It's Almost Like Being in Love

## *Romance, Hollywood-Style*

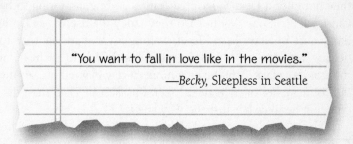

> **"You want to fall in love like in the movies."**
>
> —*Becky*, Sleepless in Seattle

Years before she hits puberty, a girl dreams about her first encounter with a boy. Will she meet her Prince Charming at a ball where he will sweep her off her feet? Perhaps she will be the beauty courted by a beast only to discover later his princelike charms. Then, of course, she could fall for someone who is "not her kind" and have to battle family and friends in a desperate attempt to save their love.

Melodramatic, to be sure, but to a young girl, fantasizing about love is the first step toward experiencing the real thing. And where does she come up with the plot lines for these love stories? Everywhere, from the TV shows and movies she watches, to the novels she reads, to the love songs she listens to, to the magazines and tabloid newspapers she devours.

Love themes have occupied writers from the time of William

Shakespeare. *Twelfth Night, Much Ado About Nothing,* and *A Midsummer Night's Dream* would merely be romps in the countryside without the passionate interplay between the sexes. Keep in mind that Romeo and Juliet were teenagers, and you can begin to understand your own modern-day adolescent who seems consumed with the soap opera called love.

We're far from the two-theater town of Will Shakespeare. Our children now live in a media-saturated world where images concerning love, romance, and, yes, sex, bombard them daily. Who will our daughters choose as their role models? Will they hope for a Disney-scripted happy ending, and long to be Cinderella or Snow White? Do they fancy themselves as Drew Barrymore in *Never Been Kissed,* waiting for that special man to declare his love by running onto a baseball field in front of thousands of fans? Will he be a modern-day Pygmalion, setting out to make her over, as in the teen hit *She's All That,* then discovering he likes her just the way she is?

Is she more sophisticated? During the heyday of *Sex and the City,* a T-shirt company produced tops with the sayings "I'm a Carrie," "I'm a Charlotte," "I'm a Miranda," and "I'm a Samantha." One mother held her breath when her fifteen-year-old daughter returned from a shopping trip with two friends and they proudly displayed their purchases. The mother recalled: "I exhaled when I realized she had chosen Charlotte," the most sexually conservative member of the famous quartet.

Pretending to be a sex siren doesn't mean your daughter is in danger of having sex in the city (or country). Generations of girls have visualized themselves as the vixen of the moment, whether Marilyn Monroe, Ursula Andress, Jane Fonda (in her *Barbarella* days), or Jennifer Lopez. Those same girls (perhaps even you?) also imagined themselves as the "good girl," spurning a Lothario's advances in order to "save themselves" until the right boy came along. (Think Ann-Margret in *Bye Bye Birdie.*)

When you see your daughter lying on her bed, staring at her ceiling with a look of contentment on her face, she could be playing back in her mind one of her own romantic fantasies. Tomorrow is the day, she thinks, when she will finally attract his attention in the lunch line. He didn't know she liked him! Now that he does, he will do anything to keep her affection. Of course, days and nights of Sturm und Drang intervene in the manner of misunderstandings, missed messages, and barriers thrown up by rivals. But in the end, love will prevail and your daughter and her beau will finally be together. Roll the credits!

Before you can review your daughter's real-life love story, you need to steep yourself in her fantasy world. That means learning about the media events and images that serve as the raw material for her production. Some of this material is PG, even G-rated, suitable for all viewing audiences. Unfortunately, more of what she is exposed to these days is rated R, restricted to those over seventeen. When she uses these racier schemes she may need some parental guidance to edit her final cut.

If you've ever scratched your head and wondered, Why is she acting that way? you will soon come up with some answers. During adolescence, your daughter will use various plots, giving each one a modern spin, as she attempts to work out her own romantic drama. Consider this chapter your primer, Adolescent Culture 101. Your homework will involve acting like your daughter—watching her on-screen love stories. So grab some popcorn, relax, and expect to be entertained, occasionally shocked, but most of all, educated.

## The Best Years of Our Lives

During one of her live concerts, Barbra Streisand talked about going to the movies as a young girl growing up in Brooklyn. The first movie she saw was the screen version of *Guys and Dolls* with Marlon Brando as Sky Masterson, the gambler persuaded to give up his criminal ways by the Bible-thumping Sarah Brown, played by Jean Simmons. Sitting there in that darkened theater, Barbra, like so many other young women, fell in love with the virile, brooding Brando.

One woman remembers the first time she fell in love with the image on the screen. "For me it was Christopher Reeve playing Superman," she recalled. "After him, I never thought anyone else would measure up." (She was wrong, finally finding and marrying her down-to-earth super man.)

Neither a teenage Streisand nor the woman who lusted after Superman stood any chance of meeting, much less landing, their screen crushes. Yet each could fantasize that she was Sarah or Lois Lane, finding her soul mate.

Who was your matinee idol? Before you assess your daughter's media world, take some time to remember how you first fell in love in the movies. Don't be embarrassed. You're not alone. Millions of Americans do it every year and have for a long, long time. Reviewing your own history will put you in the proper mind-set to screen your daughter's favorite flicks. Here are some things you can do.

**Rent the movie that started it all.** Come on. You remember the movie that first set your young heart on fire. Was it *Casablanca*? *Gone With the Wind*? *Pretty in Pink*? *When Harry Met Sally*? Maybe even an animated classic like *Sleeping Beauty*. Perhaps one actor captured your attention—Sean Connery, as the sexy and indestructible James Bond, with his encyclopedic knowledge about everything from guns and explosives to diamonds and wine; Tom Cruise, lip-syncing in his underwear or displaying his killer smile; or Harrison Ford, as Indiana Jones, the world-renowned archeologist battling the evil Nazis, yet revealing his vulnerability and fear of snakes.

**Watch it by yourself.** Turn out the lights and try to remember what it was like viewing that movie as a young adolescent. Did you go to the movie alone? With a parent? A group of friends? Did you share your secret crush with them or hold it close to your heart?

**Visualize your room.** Did your adolescent fantasy spill over onto your bedroom walls? Whose face dominated the posters in your room? Did you close your eyes at night hoping one of these idols would play a starring role in your dreams?

**Analyze your attraction.** What quality or characteristic served as a magnet to pull you toward your screen crush? Was that element purely physical? Don't apologize. Who could resist Denzel Washington's grin or Johnny Depp's soulful eyes? Was it the attitude displayed by the star? Richard Gere's arrogant swagger or John Travolta's swiveling hips?

Was your fascination based on something deeper and more meaningful? Did you fall in love despite the actor's crooked teeth or less-than-Adonis-like physique? Did you like his voice and imagine him calling your name? Did you see true intelligence behind his less-than-perfect looks and imagine that he would surely understand your angst and do anything he could to help you survive friends, school, and parents?

## From Here to Maturity

Now the hard part: What role did this movie fantasy play in your real life? Did you spend your school hours walking the halls, searching in vain for a middle-school boy who closely resembled your movie star hunk? Did you truly believe that you would come home after school one day and find Michael J. Fox or Paul Newman sitting in your living room? Did you turn down dates with friends or even with boys so that you could wait by the phone for your film lover to call?

No! Your fantasy life remained separate, a private compartment where you stored away your adolescent dreams. Those musings may have found physical life in a diary that you kept under lock and key. But you knew that Rob Lowe wasn't going to magically appear to take you to the prom.

You may not have thought about the subject, but your film fantasies:

**Elevated your expectations.** Film heroes did something extraordinary to land the girl of their dreams. Perhaps the hero you settled on didn't save the world from nuclear war, but he may have rescued your cat from a tree or helped your father change a tire. Chances are he pulled out your chair when you went to a restaurant or let you have the bigger half of the umbrella when it rained. You expected special treatment after being spoiled by your film star.

**Stoked the flames of passion.** When Cary Grant kissed Grace Kelly in *To Catch a Thief,* fireworks exploded in the background, a none too subtle hint that an explosion of another kind was occurring. When Tom Hanks took Meg Ryan's hand in *Sleepless in Seattle,* she felt the "magic" feeling that had been lacking in her relationship with her fiancé. When did you feel those magical fireworks in your own relationships? Perhaps that boyfriend was a flash in the pan, but for a while he made you feel special and you knew you could never settle for less.

**Provided role models.** Which film starlet did you long to be? Audrey Hepburn as the offbeat Holly Golightly? Meg Ryan, the cynic who bad-mouths love yet manages to find it before the end of each movie? Molly Ringwald? Ali MacGraw? Natalie Wood? These characters must do something right because they always get their man. Allowing ourselves to imitate their actions gives us a starting point.

**Increased your relationship vocabulary.** What would a good movie be without a great script? And why should all those words remain lost on the screen? Film dialogue that is smart, witty, and rings true soon enters our lexicon. Perhaps your boyfriend never said, "Here's looking at you, kid," but he may have used less-quoted lines. More important, however, just listening to actors talk through their problems on the screen probably gave you some strategies for talking through your own later on.

**Occupied your time.** As Charlotte York once exclaimed on *Sex and the City,* "I've been dating for fifteen years. Where is he?" Waiting for Mr. Right to come along can be agonizing, yet the pain can be made less sharp when you can retreat now and then into your dreams.

Now that you have taken a trip down movie memory lane, let's move on to the present and your daughter. Like you, she is taking some of her romantic cues from what she sees on the silver screen. But her movies and role models have changed.

## Down with Love

Doris Day and Rock Hudson were the most popular onscreen romantic couple of their day, frolicking through a string of hits (*Pillow Talk, Lover Come Back,* and *Send Me No Flowers*). The plots were repetitive (revolving around the battle of the sexes), their characters stereotypical (Doris was the virgin, Rock the playboy), and the twist usually involved a case of mistaken identity (guaranteed to bring the two together). In 2003, Peyton Reed decided to spoof those movies and directed *Down with Love,* starring Renée Zellweger and Ewan McGregor. From the dazzling set designs to the 1960s period clothes to the split-screen phone conversations, a staple in the earlier films, *Down with Love,* the critics agreed, captured the fun of the original Doris Day–Rock Hudson romps. However, *Down with Love* failed to capture something it desperately sought—the youth audience. Producers soon discovered that most young people had never seen the earlier films and therefore couldn't understand that the new movie was a satire.

On its own, *Down with Love* was panned by young people. One teenage girl in her online review called the movie "piffle light." She added: "It's so cute, you can't stand watching it for more than five minutes."

Young people, for the most part, have moved past their parents' movies. "There are more sophisticated and adult themes in teen movies today because kids are more sophisticated than they used to be," according to Jim Gillespie, who did the makeup for *Sixteen Candles* and directed the seminal *I Know What You Did Last Summer.* Gillespie told a reporter from the *Bergen Record* (NJ): "The teen market won't stand to be condescended to."

When did teenagers become savvier and turn toward edgier fare? Nick Clooney, George's father and the author of *The Movies That Changed Us,* points to the 1967 film *The Graduate,* which starred Dustin Hoffman as a recent college graduate seduced by an older woman, the sultry, smoldering Anne Bancroft. Clooney studied more than a thousand movies and found that before 1967, 30 percent, excluding musicals, could be categorized as romantic movies. After 1967, that number falls to about 11 percent.

Did romance suddenly fall out of fashion? Not at all. In the 1960s and '70s, however, young people were protesting an unpopular war and fairy-tale endings seemed out of place. Succeeding generations, too, turned away from the frothy, lighthearted fare that their parents embraced. Increasingly, young people wanted their love stories told with a heavy dose of reality thrown in. In the new millennium, movies aimed at a youthful audience are racier than ever. Here are some ways the movies your daughter watches differ from the films of your youth:

**More violence.** A good example is Baz Luhrmann's 1996 retelling of *Romeo and Juliet,* with Leonardo DiCaprio and Claire Danes playing the star-crossed lovers, complete with gangs, bullets, and plenty of on-screen violence. The movie, panned by most critics, was a hit with the audience that mattered most—adolescents.

Of course, there was violence in the original Shakespeare

play, with both Romeo and Juliet killing themselves in the end. Graphic violence, however, is a modern invention. With Hollywood's special effects, some movies that begin as love stories wind up as horror flicks because of all the blood and gore.

**MTV influence.** Forget those melodic, sweeping musical scores of the past. Movie sound tracks now are filled with heavy metal and rap. Eminem's movie, *8 Mile,* featured his controversial rap songs throughout. Even though the movie was rated R, many young people saw it when it came out on DVD. Eminem is only one of many rap artists who have made the crossover from music to film, thus increasing their influence.

**Sexually explicit scenes.** Once the lovebirds kissed, moviemakers used to "fade to black," leaving the audience to imagine what happened next. One movie critic compiled a list of the Top Ten Movie Kisses of All Time. Discovering that all the kisses were from vintage-classic films, he observed: "Now they skip the kisses to go straight to the R-rated things. Somehow it was more romantic in the old movies."

These days, very little is left to the imagination. And while sexual shenanigans usually earn a picture an R-rating, many PG-13 movies contain nudity. (Jack Nicholson, for example, bared his backside, while Diane Keaton showed her breasts in the PG-13–rated *Something's Gotta Give.*)

**Revamped classics.** Looking around for material, directors often decide to film a classic. Yet a straight telling of the story will never do. Thus, the recent film versions of Nathaniel Hawthorne's *The Scarlet Letter* and Charles Dickens's *Great Expectations,* included plenty of sex and nudity. Both, incidentally, are rated R.

## Separating Fantasy from Reality

Princesses and prom queens still show up on the silver screen in movies that are rated PG or PG-13. While older teens eschew these films, young adolescents often have no choice if they want to go to the movies with their friends. An adolescent has to be seventeen or older to get into an R-rated film (or else be accompanied by a parent or guardian) and many movie theaters are strictly enforcing the rule. Later, when an R-rated film comes out on DVD or is shown on pay-TV, mom and dad have to do the policing.

There's not much new under the sun, and so upbeat teen movies still depend on the tried and true plot devices to get boy and girl together. Script writers rely on the happy ending. For the most part, parents applaud these movies. And why not? These flicks avoid explicit sex and gratuitous violence, preferring instead to tug at the audience's heart strings with a warm-hearted and familiar story. Parents see these movies as safe, harmless entertainment.

There is one caveat, however. Keep in mind that your daughter may have a hard time separating the fantasy she sees on the screen from the reality of her own life. In adolescent love land, happy endings are few and far between. Why is it that these starlets always manage to wind up with the boy of their dreams when your daughter can't even work up the courage to talk to her crush?

One teenage girl we interviewed agreed. "Girls are obsessed with finding their soul mate," she said, attributing that longing to the fairy-tale themed movies, like *A Walk to Remember,* popular with teens. One mother added that her daughter's favorite movies have romantic themes—*The Wedding Planner, Two Weeks' Notice*—and she worries her daughter's expectations will never be met by the real boys she dates.

After you watch a movie together, a little discussion may help her to understand that Hollywood-style endings rarely happen, even to the stars themselves. Point out that famous fairy-tale couple Brad Pitt and Jennifer Aniston, for instance, failed to keep their marriage together. Relationship struggles are common in off-screen Hollywood. A columnist from the *Mirror,* a London newspaper, researched the cast of the popular film *Love Actually* to see if their real-life romances were as successful as their on-screen ones. He concluded: "In real life, many of the blockbuster's big names have endured a rocky road to true romance—with a string of lonely nights, divorces, and stormy break-ups behind them."

Some fantasy on the screen can have even more harmful effects. Near the end of *Pretty Woman,* Vivian, the kind-hearted hooker (Julia Roberts in her star-making role), turns down a proposal made by the rich financier played by Richard Gere to become a kept woman. Surprised, he asks Vivian what she wants. "I want the fairy tale," she tells him.

*Pretty Woman* is a fairy tale itself, an updated version of Cinderella, Pygmalion—take your pick. Are there young girls who truly believe they can run away from home, become a street walker, and find someone who is handsome and rich to rescue them? It seems so. When Oprah Winfrey broadcast a show on teenage prostitutes, spotlighting the violent, dark world they inhabit, one of them said through her tears, "It's nothing like *Pretty Woman.*"

Movies are powerful. What we see on the screen can get us thinking, even change our opinions. After its release in 1997, James Cameron's *Titanic* became a phenomenon. But people didn't just storm the movie. Record numbers of travelers booked cruises to experience life on a large ocean liner. Steven Spielberg's *Saving Private Ryan* led to a new appreciation of the men and women who died in World War II and ultimately to the creation of a long-overdue memorial in Washington, DC. So don't dismiss the effect movies can have on your daughter's emerging romantic sensibilities. She is watching, so you should be, too.

## Make It a Blockbuster Night

Talking to a young adolescent about relationships and romance is a daunting task. Both you and your daughter may be embarrassed by the subject matter. You may have trouble bringing up the topic in a casual way that will get her talking. You may have concerns about your daughter's social life. Perhaps she is moving too fast; perhaps not moving at all. How can you have a meaningful conversation without scaring her away?

Watch a movie together. "The movies are a wonderful way to open up a dialogue between parents and children," says Gary Solomon in his book *The Motion Picture Prescription*. Solomon, who uses movies in his therapy with patients, believes that movies can be employed as a valuable parenting tool. "If either you or your children have difficulty talking about a particular problem, the movies can be used to create foundation for future discussion," he says.

To get you started, we have compiled a list of twelve movies that you can watch with your daughter. Some are vintage, others are more current. They are all award winners in their own right, so don't worry about being bored. You may have seen many of them before, but chances are viewing these movies with your daughter will cause you to see them in a new light. Your daughter may have seen some of the newer movies, and, no doubt, will be excited to narrate as you go along. We've provided some starting points for dialogue, but you will probably come up with lots of ideas of your own.

Don't lecture your daughter throughout the movie, or she will avoid watching anything with you in the future. Relax and she will, too. You may want to wait until the following day to ask what she thought. If you selected well, the movie will probably strike a nerve and she will want to open up to you. That's an award-winning moment.

## Twelve Movies to Watch with Your Daughter

**Beauty and the Beast** Besides a great musical score and the singing talents of Jerry Orbach and Angela Lansbury, this animated Disney classic has an important message even a small child can understand: judge people not by their looks, but by what's inside. Underneath the Beast's gruff exterior lurks a kind heart. Even though the Beast has riches, his gift to Beauty is a library filled with books, a counterpoint to today's materialistic youth culture. (Rated G)

**Casablanca** Love never happens in a vacuum. Outside events, either on a local or global scale, have a nasty way of intervening. No movie brings home this point like the classic *Casablanca,* starring two film legends, Humphrey Bogart and Ingrid Bergman. Rick and Ilsa's timing couldn't have been worse, falling in love in Paris just as the Nazis invade the city. When Ilsa fails to meet Rick at the train station, sending him a cryptic farewell note, he assumes he's been jilted. The two meet again during the war at Rick's Café Americain in Casablanca, Morocco, and have the chance to rekindle their romance. Yet, in one of the most famous movie lines ever, Rick tells the now-married Ilsa, "It doesn't take much to see that the problems of three little people don't amount to a hill of beans in this crazy world." Adolescents tend to be self-absorbed, never more so than when they are "in love." This movie will help you launch a conversation about how the outside world and family matter too. (Not rated)

**How to Marry a Millionaire** Adolescents are growing up in a materialistic society. Somehow love has become commercialized, too. Announcement of a star's engagement often includes details on her multicarat diamond ring and the wedding celebration that is sure to hit seven, even eight figures. So why not set your sights high and plan to marry Donald Trump or another wealthy man? This movie stars three of Hollywood's femme fatales—Marilyn Monroe, Lauren Bacall, and Betty Grable—working as models in New York City and setting out to trap rich men. Their plan, however, backfires. Monroe and Grable marry working stiffs, while Bacall marries her "gas pump jockey," only to later discover he is the real thing—a millionaire. True love, it turns out, doesn't have a price tag. Something young people need to know. (Not rated)

***Pretty in Pink*** Molly Ringwald plays Andie, a girl from the wrong side of the tracks who gets asked to the school dance by Blane, a rich classmate played by Andrew McCarthy. Friends on both sides drive a wedge between the two young lovers. (Andie's friend, Duckie, played by Jon Cryer, is in love with her, while Blane's friend, played by James Spader, is a snob.) This movie provides plenty of fodder for discussing class differences, the negative influence of friends, and loyalty to those who care about us. (Rated PG-13)

***She's All That*** When school star Zach gets dumped by the popular Taylor, he finds himself without a date for the prom. He bets his friend that he can take any girl in the school and make her over to be an acceptable date. As fate has it, the first girl who walks in, Laney (Rachel Leigh Cook), presents a challenge. An artist who takes care of her father and brother, Laney has no time for prissiness or proms. But she agrees to go out with Zach and soon finds there's more substance to him than she thought. In the end, she's pitted against the vacuous Taylor for prom queen. If your daughter is feeling like a misfit in her school, this movie could help you broach that topic and show her that there are boys who will look beyond superficial things like popularity. (Rated PG-13)

***10 Things I Hate About You*** If only William Shakespeare knew he had penned so many stories for teens! This movie is an updated *Taming of the Shrew*. Julia Stiles plays the sullen Kate, who has sworn off boys, while her sister, the sunny

Bianca, can't wait to date. When the girls' father decrees that Bianca can't date until Kate does, a plot is hatched. Enter Patrick Verona (Heath Ledger) who agrees to woo Kate for a fee. Of course, he will eventually fall for her and in the process melt her steely exterior. If your teen has read the Shakespeare play, she will have fun pointing out the amusing nods to the original (the high school is named Padua). Beyond that, you can have a discussion on how a thin line often separates love and hate, and that she shouldn't judge a boy until she gets to know him better. (Rated PG-13)

**The Notebook**  This movie, adapted from the bestselling book by Nicholas Sparks, will have you and your daughter discussing the fact that true love conquers all. The basic plot is not original. Noah, the son of a dirt-poor father, and Allie, the daughter of wealthy parents, meet and fall in love. Her family is appalled and ship her off to college. Working as a volunteer nurse during World War II, she meets a young army officer who is more her social equal. They become engaged. Will Noah and Allie ever get together? We know perhaps from the start since the beginning of the movie features two elderly people in a nursing home, the aging Noah, reading from the notebook to Allie, now suffering from dementia. The story in the notebook unfolds as he reads and the movie flashes back. Along the way we learn the whole story. The movie spotlights how love can survive even the cruelest separation, whether physical or mental. (Rated PG-13, with some lovemaking scenes)

**The Princess Diaries**  Based on the popular book by Meg Cabot, this movie follows the school geek as she discovers she is really a princess. She undergoes the necessary transformation from ugly duckling to swan, but that metamorphosis is just the surface of the story. The fledgling princess learns the value of true friendship and discovers those who truly love her have loved her all the time, tiara or not. (Rated G)

**The Way We Were** Sometimes no matter how hard a couple tries, different philosophies doom their relationship. Hubbell, played by Robert Redford, is a gifted writer, but he's willing to sacrifice his principles to make it as a screenwriter in 1950s Hollywood. Katie, played by Barbra Streisand, is an activist who stands by her convictions. Despite their differences, the two fall in love. When the McCarthy witchhunt pits them against each other, their marriage falls apart. Katie returns to New York and remarries. Handing out pamphlets for yet another cause, Katie runs into Hubbell in front of the Plaza Hotel. In that brief meeting, their love is palpable. Yet both know that love alone is not enough. This movie is a great one for bringing home the point that relationships are complicated and go beyond physical attraction. (Rated PG)

**13 Going on 30** Who wouldn't want to skip over all those awkward teen years and find herself a beautiful, successful adult? Jenna, thanks to some magical wishing dust, does. But like the old saying goes, "Be careful what you wish for." Jenna discovers that in the intervening seventeen years she wasn't such a nice person and rose to the top by stepping on others, including her best friend from childhood, Matt. While Tom Hanks did a better job with this theme in *Big*, Jennifer Garner as Jenna allows us to see this story from the girl's point of view. You can launch many discussions after watching this one, including the price of popularity. (Rated PG-13)

**West Side Story** Whether you watch the movie or take your daughter to see a stage production, *West Side Story* is still the best retelling of Romeo and Juliet ever made. Tony and Maria never stand a chance of having their love survive when faced with such hate and prejudice from both their families and their friends. Whether or not your daughter is dating someone of a different background, this movie will give you plenty to talk about. Could this happen today? How could a better ending be written today? (Not rated)

**Win a Date with Tad Hamilton** Your daughter probably daydreams about meeting her teen idol. In this movie, Rosalee, played with a naïve sweetness by Kate Bosworth, does, and, more than that, captures his heart. She discovers that despite Hamilton's screen image, just like the rest of us, he is searching for true love. This movie can help you bring your starstruck daughter back down to earth. In the end, Rosalee finds that her true love was right before her all the time. (Rated PG-13)

# CHAPTER 4

# You've Got to Have Friends

*Girlfriends' Guide to Love and Lacerations*

> The word *friends* doesn't stretch big enough to describe how we feel about each other. We forget where one of us starts and the other one stops.
>
> —*Lena, of* The Sisterhood of the Traveling Pants *fame*

A girl forges intense friendships with other girls during early adolescence. The operative word here is *intense*. Some shop for necklaces for one another, a popular example being two halves of a heart inscribed with best friends status. Preteens seemingly joined at the hip don't have to advertise their closeness on T-shirts because everyone at middle school knows who hangs out with whom. Pick up a typical eighth-grade yearbook and, in all likelihood, pictorials of inseparable pairs smile out of the pages.

Female twosomes, threesomes, and packs form highly emotional pacts. Girls stick exclusively with one another in school, trade secrets in the cafeteria, and pass notes constantly throughout the day. They text a shorthand of intimacy during the daylight hours. After stepping off the school bus at home, they pick up electronically where they left off minutes ago.

Like all candid, honest self-disclosures, these confidences build bonds. As young adolescent girls define themselves by and with these connections, they begin a female brand of connectedness that comes naturally and fundamentally to women. Sometimes these relationships almost seem like love affairs, without the sexual connotations of course. A mother reminisced, "I think back on my eighth-grade best friend and me—I am slightly embarrassed by us in hindsight. Our relationship was more like a later life romance. We wrote extensive notes to each other every night, talked on the phone endlessly, 'died' when we couldn't hang out together on weekends."

Don't you know exactly what she means? We do. Such bonds of affection can be a double-edged sword. Young girls rally and restore one another, and yet risk being affected by a dark side of female competitiveness and even cruelty. Few girls survive their tweenage peer connections without a laceration or two straight to their heart.

In this section it will become clear what girls gain from intense female bonding and how these formative early relationships forecast the positive qualities of friendship that girls can later reclaim as women. Many girls suffer at the hands of mean girls. They may pick up self-sabotaging ideas about relationships and these toxic themes may harm their romances with boys. As we delve into this phenomenon, we will offer a few guidelines so you can minister to your daughter's scars and make sure any emotional hits are only temporary.

## Laverne and Shirley, Lizzie McGuire and Miranda, Sisterhoods Forever

A girl of ten or eleven expects closeness and companionship, empathy and safety, from her girlfriends. Every friend wants to be able to trust her favorite buddy and all the girls in her circle. In classic television sitcoms and dramas through the years, wacky or wickedly sophisticated pairs scored big ratings with female viewers: Lucy and Ethel, Cagney and Lacey, Mary and Rhoda, and on and on. Books, such as the bestselling series beginning with *The Sisterhood of the Traveling Pants,* starring fifteen-year-olds Lena, Tibby, Bridget, and Carmen, delight armies of female readers. Plotlines of female buddy tales affirm that friendship is *the* how-to guide for surviving life and especially adolescence.

Within fictional and real friendship, tween girls share their innermost secrets and insecurities. Such disclosure is often a first as this tends to be the first time in a girl's life that she reveals private stuff to someone other than a sister, brother, or parent. The details and dramas of her family circumstances are whispered in the dark at sleepovers or traded behind closed bedroom doors.

Parents may not be privy to these confidential exchanges, but they do sense how the stock of their daughter's girlfriends rises. It is not uncommon for a mother to feel nostalgic, even hurt somewhere along the way by a daughter's obvious preference for her favorite peers. Such preoccupation with friends is normal. Journeying away from home earmarks the separation process that children begin during middle school. This path of escalating independence ends in early adulthood.

In the best of these heady times, girlfriends give one another exactly what each needs in the bargain, namely understanding, companionship, acceptance, and loyalty. A girl longs to be known and understood by others. She seeks comrades with whom she can explore hobbies, activities, or interests. The sense of belonging that is highly valued by ten- to fifteen-year-olds is found within a close-knit bevy of girls. And finally, girls on the cusp of adolescence, which dangles so much change and uncertainty, long for trust and security. Friends should stick by them no matter what. These are all positive learning experiences about the value of camaraderie.

Before we wrote our first book on preteens, we quizzed children between the ages of ten and fifteen in all fifty states and nearly all eight Canadian provinces. We wanted to know what friendship meant and what it delivered to these real-life experts. Forty-three percent of our sampling believed that a friend should be nice and a good listener. Twenty-nine percent wanted someone to do things with. Fifteen percent specifically underlined trust, claiming a friend should keep your secrets.

Girlfriends contribute to one another's understanding of boys and how romances unfold and unravel. They serve as sounding boards. A girl with a circle of friends, or even one good pal, has a willing audience to talk through a crush. "Do you think he likes me?" Friends become a private review board, and can give opinions on a boy and if he is worthy. "If you had seen him backing away from Lily—she obviously wanted to flirt and he didn't." Girls serve as one another's reference points as to what is normal at this stage of romantic games. They can gauge their strong feelings of joy or heartache by comparing them with what their buddies experience. This can be very nurturing and positive.

Unfortunately, young adolescent friendships aren't 100 percent beneficial. At this age, girls can undermine each other as well.

## The Backstabbers: With a Smile on Her Face

After publishing our findings we went on to develop half a dozen books on this age group. And we spent a number of years working online as parenting experts specializing in young and older adolescent issues on iVillage's Parent Soup and Time Warner's ParentTime. As cyber versions of Ann Landers and Dear Abby we clicked with girls and listened to their mothers. One of the most common issues that came our way turned out to be friendships. When it came to the outpourings on friends, 99 percent of the time the tales told of pain and betrayal.

Here is one of hundreds of missives from a mother who feels disturbed and disgusted by her thirteen-year-old daughter:

I thought that I already lived through trying times with my oldest daughter, but that was a piece of cake compared to what I am going through with my Michelle. Michelle is popular in school—too much so, I think. Dozens of calls ring over our home telephone per night. When she has friends over, she makes them do her chores (and taunts them if they don't) while she chats on the phone or the Internet with others. If I tell her that she is behaving rudely, she's nasty to me. What's the matter with my Michelle, and with all those others who reward her when she acts like this?!

Large numbers of girls fall on the receiving end of nasty treatment from other girls, ranging from being used, sniggered at, and stabbed in the back. Girlworld, though, doesn't divide up neatly into mean girls and good girls. Even good girls on occasion victimize their peers and their friends with mean-spirited remarks or subtle putdowns from cold shoulders to eye-rolling. While some girls with a friend or two may stay outside of all this, the majority can't and don't. Why?

The answer lies partly in the developmental deficits of all young adolescents. They need so much to belong. They are so worried about falling out of favor and being accepted. Friendship is like their currency. Girls at times use and exploit this fragility. Some punish by withholding friendship or by taking it away entirely, which is called shunning or scapegoating. Since the fear of being without friends or unliked stalks so many in the stage of separating from home, girls buckle. Few stand up to rude behavior. They take it.

Ironically, being mean and intimidating can go so far that the perpetrator becomes popular. California psychologist Jaana Juvonen and her colleagues surveyed 2,000 sixth-graders. They discovered that teasers and tormentors rated as among the most liked and respected kids in school. A similar finding pertaining specifically to boys came from Duke University. Researchers there surveyed fourth- to sixth-grade boys and found one third of boys who started fights and arguments were re-warded, not ostracized, for being aggressive.

Do bullying girls or aggressive boys stay on top because kids admire them or because kids are afraid of them? Probably the latter most often. Whatever happened to the kindly Miss Con-geniality of yesterday's homecoming queens? What kind of a social system rewards nasty boys and girls? Apparently the one our daughters live in. Whether cowardice or an eroding ethical standard is at the root of popular mean queens, putting others down has been misconstrued as a way to win friends and influence people. Girls like Michelle grab power and wield it with intimidating bravado. The girls in her posse take on subordinating wishy-washy roles and will do anything, suffer any blow, to keep in her good graces.

Preadolescent malicious mayhem among girls has made newspaper headlines in the last few years by way of a new term, *relational aggression,* used to describe this tendency in girls. The new breed of analysts blames social conditioning. According to this line of reasoning, until the age of four girls are permitted to express their anger just like boys. They can get away with hitting or snarling. As they grow, however, girls are held to a stricter and more repressed standard: no hitting when you are angry. Be ladylike; be nice; be nurturing. The message often goes further: no anger, period. Of course, there are exceptions, but the usual social instructions conveyed give girls less freedom to act out: Don't put your dukes up the way boys can on the playground. The more girls are conditioned not to act out anger, the more it comes out sideways and in subtle, devious ways.

Take a moment and see if your daughter expresses her anger. How does she do so? Are you like an apparent majority of adults who remind her that girls are nice, not aggressive like boys?

Boys themselves play a huge part in the way girls misbehave and mistreat their peers and friends. Girls compete for boys' favor. A certain boy may be a pawn or he may be a prize. He might not even know that he's being homed in on or used to humiliate a girl. The boy-driven plotlines are endless. Watch for them. For instance, a girl may break up with a boy and be enraged that he pays attention to her best friend. Girls make a play for someone else's boyfriend on purpose. A shy girl may talk to the wrong boy with no evil intent and get in trouble. Rumors are spread that a girl's heartthrob walked someone else home after school. Or that a girl hooked up with someone when she didn't.

Sneaky schemes and snide gossip frequently, and with precision, strike at the heart of friendships. The Internet has become a major delivery system, as you'll see in chapter 10. Friendships get fractured. Packs break up and make up.

Many movies for the teenage audience feature mean girls, popular cliques, and girls being sacrificed in the in-crowd wars. In *Mean Girls* a new girl in school gets intoxicated by running with the mean girls. Look at *A Walk to Remember, She's All That, The Princess Diaries,* and *Drive Me Crazy.* All of these (and surely you can add to the list if you keep up with the box office for teens) are cinematic parables of what goes on socially. Popular girls are pretty and petty, accomplished and arrogant. Nice girls are used and abused. By the time the credits roll in most of these movies, the nasty girls lose the guy, or mend their ways, or are portrayed as more sensitive deep down inside. Still, girls caught in these daily dramas don't see them wrapped up fairly in two hours as happens in a movie or TV show. They see that nice girls don't always finish first in real life in seventh grade. It will take time, maturity, and parental guidance for them to digest that.

One more thought to mull over is that the tenor of our popular culture in general has deteriorated. We live in a society where humiliation serves as entertainment on TV. In the space of a generation we've gone from Phil Donahue to Jerry Springer, from audiences who wanted to embrace controversy to audience members who want to slug each other over controversy. Judge Judy and all of the other tele-justices dole out insults along with verdicts to injured victims who stand before them. Ratings blockbusters from any given television season, such as *The Apprentice* or *Survivor,* celebrate putting people down or out. Exclusion serves as story line. Our young people are affected by what they see.

## Toxic Messages Are in the Air

Girls are partly at the mercy of their insecure nature and partly caught in a toxic cultural climate. When girlfriends hurt each other or see it happening all around them they can pick up harmful messages about relationships. They can confuse what is appropriate and inappropriate.

Timing affects what girls ingest about relationships, too. Girls discover the opposite sex at about the same time that they embrace these intense emotional affairs with one another. The feelings they have, what they observe, and the scars from girlfriends—all this can carry over. Being shunned can wound their self-esteem. Seeing bad girls win even temporarily can color lessons about how the world works and how love works.

Girls can internalize their experiences, the positive aspects of friendships and the negative ones. Reams of confessionals have passed our desk over the last decade. As you read on, recognize these dangerous ideas girls can get from others around them and from the muddled social landscape.

### A Love-Hate Rhythm Exists in Relationships

The mother of a seventh-grader says:

> I need advice ASAP! My daughter, Sarah, has had a conflict every other week with certain girlfriends. They are manipulative and controlling. I know Sarah plays a part in all this. The girls all fight one day and then the next day they are friends again. My Sarah's always been a leader, a good student, and very creative and driven. Now

her grades are slipping and I get notices that her class behavior is disruptive—too much talking and note-passing. She does not want me to get involved, but watching this is so very hard!

Girls are good buddies one day and enemies the next. The day after that, the girls are friends again. A revolving door pattern of emotional flip-flopping describes countless young girls. In the squabbles, misunderstandings, and deliberate machinations, girls incur social distress regularly. Hurt and relief alternately vacillate on a daily, even hourly basis. Feelings of love and hate take turns.

*Girls can assume this is par for the course for all future relationships.*

## The Language Spoken Includes Verbal Abuse

Aghast, this mother makes a shameful confession:

I have a thirteen-year-old daughter in eighth grade. I overheard my child talking to one of her friends about verbally abusing another student. From what she said, it sounded as though this was *not* the first time that she and her friends had done this. I spoke to her afterwards and she said, "But it's fun!" She doesn't think that being truly hurtful to a child just for the "fun" of it is wrong!

Words of ridicule are levied inside and outside a girl's circle of friends. Many a girl has been on the receiving end of remarks like "Oh those pants make you look so fat—just kidding." Fatso, slut—overt insults are bad enough. The subtle ones are even worse because they are confusing. Girls wonder: Should I take the insult personally or let it go? Respect and dignity are hard to find as verbal abuse becomes part of girl-to-girl rapport.

*Girls can mistakenly conclude that friendship can be nice or incredibly hurtful.*

## Possessiveness Is Nine Tenths of the Law

The next mother learned how kindness brings with it a kick:

> In fourth grade, my daughter Beth befriended a girl that
> no one liked particularly. Beth said, So what! She liked
> Amy just fine. I had always taught my daughter to be
> kind. Then a new girl came into the picture and that
> made three. Soon this new friend said she wanted my
> daughter to be only her friend. Beth refused to drop Amy.
> Her new friend retaliated by spreading lies about Beth,
> claiming my daughter held a stick to her throat. This
> little villain got her younger sister to agree to this
> outlandish accusation. They harassed my daughter. We
> wound up in the principal's office.

Beth is caught in the *be my friend only or else* stranglehold. *If
you are her friend then you can't be mine.* Possessiveness and jealousy reign.

*Girls can come away confused about loyalty and freedom.*

## Friendship Leads to Loneliness

This mother's antenna shot up:

> Last night my twelve-year-old daughter, Kristin, and I at-
> tended a high school basketball game. At half time, my
> daughter and her middle school basketball teammates were
> scheduled to be introduced. Sitting across the gym from us,
> I watched my child's best friend snub her. When my daugh-
> ter went to sit next to her, the girl got up and walked away
> with other girls in tow. Kristin skulked back to me.
>
> When I questioned her, Kristin insisted this snubbing
> was no big deal. When I probed how often this kind of
> thing happens, Kristin insisted it didn't bother her and I
> was creating an issue where there was none. What I saw
> hurt and I hurt for her. I guess my question is this: Am I

overreacting? Is this normal seventh-grade stuff? Should I be concerned when my daughter apparently is not?

The answer is yes. A best friend should not snub a best friend. Doing so in private is painful enough. Public humiliation adds to the injury.

When a girl denies that being snubbed hurts, she is swallowing her hurt. According to a University of California at Los Angeles study done by social psychologist Matt Lieberman, a snub affects the brain the same way that visceral pain does. It's as if someone punches you in the stomach. The experiment behind this conclusion featured thirteen volunteers playing a computer game of ball. Certain players were denied participation in this virtual catch. Desperately, the excluded players claimed they were ready to play. The distress over being rejected registered in the same part of the brain where physical pain sensations are recorded.

*Girls can conclude from shunning and being shunned that sometimes friendship is akin to loneliness and even humiliation.*

## Relationships Render Girls Speechless

This next mother explains a more permanent snub.

My daughter, Cheyenne, will turn thirteen in May. For the past two months she's been having problems with a girl, formerly her best friend for the last five years. This best buddy, Anna, suddenly wants to hang with the in-crowd, and has left Cheyenne behind. My husband thinks I am blowing things out of proportion here. After school, Cheyenne spends all her time alone and very quiet. She won't talk to me about any of this—how she feels or what she's said to her former best friend.

Throughout middle school, girls grow and change. It's not uncommon for friends like Cheyenne and Anna to outgrow one another. One becomes more focused on boys; the other still plays with dolls. Girls do not have the tools or the tact automatically to resolve growing apart graciously or gracefully. So girls move on callously and reject former friends, leaving the left-behind child dumbfounded, speechless, suffering in silence.

*Girls learn that relationships can be too painful for words. Some don't talk because they can't articulate what is happening to them. They can't fathom what they did to deserve such treatment. Others are too embarrassed and run from discussions.*

## Love Has No Pride

The mother of this twelve-year-old grapples with the aftermath of her child's rejection:

> I have a daughter, Tiffany, who is going through a lot. Tiffany and Sue were best friends. Lately, Sue has been very cruel to Tiff. My daughter has been writing her poems and making her tapes in the hopes of trying to understand why Sue doesn't like her anymore and to change Sue's mind. Tiffany is devastated. I hear that Sue trashes my daughter all over town. I want my daughter to get through this and move on, but what do I say?

Middle schoolers know that rejected girlfriends will try anything to turn back the clock. Rather than focus on personal dignity in order to break away and heal, girls opt for groveling.

*Girls are vulnerable to believing that love has no pride. This leads to self-sabotaging decision making.*

In conclusion, those are merely a few bad lessons that typically surround tweenage girls. You may have observed others. The way that girls act out their friendship stories reminds us of the old rhyme about a girl: When she is good she is very, very good and when she is bad she is horrid. Debilitating social experiences coexist alongside the nurturing ones during middle school. Girls are at risk of becoming handicapped in the relationship department by negative messages unless parents step up to the plate. It's a good idea to get into the habit of watching for such potentially toxic lessons.

*The leap from letting a friend treat you badly to allowing a boyfriend to do likewise is not very far.*

## He's a Coldhearted Snake: The Rise of Manhandling Creeps

A body of data exists that affirms how more and more teenage girls tolerate being manhandled by abusive young men.

- Approximately one in five girls between the ages of fourteen and eighteen are the victims of dating aggression, according to 2004 statistics from the pages of the *Journal of the American Medical Association.*
- More than half of the restraining orders filed by teenagers in Massachusetts in 1994 were against abusive ex-boyfriends, according to the state department of probation.
- Tampa Bay, Florida, activist Cathy Capo Stone introduced a program called Love Shouldn't Hurt for their community after handling three hundred cases of domestic violence in 2003, insisting the target audience needed to be middle schoolers. Why? Apparently the sixteen to twenty-four age group accounted for the majority of the cases.
- A Westchester County, New York, symposium drawing 270 teenagers surveyed attendees and found that one third reported having been hit, two fifths knew someone who was an abuser, and three fifths knew someone who was being abused in their dating relationship.
- Santa Clara County, California, opened the first Juvenile

Domestic and Family Violence Court to handle rising numbers of teen cases. Debbie Licurse, coordinator for the Center for Human Development of San Jose, California, comments, "One of the greatest observations I've had among teens is the minimization of emotional abuse, using terms such as 'bitch' and not being able to communicate one's feelings. The only emotion I hear from boys and girls is 'I'm pissed off. I'm angry and upset.' They need to expand their vocabulary on feeling words and express those feelings, but they don't know how to do it."

North, south, east, west and in between—if you look for episodes and warnings about dating violence, they abound. A seventeen-year-old high school senior girl from Cross River, New York, said, "I can name four of my friends who have been in abusive relationships and I've seen how they escalate. There's a lot of emotional and mental abuse going on."

What's even more disturbing than all the reports of abusive romances is the apparent acceptance of manhandling. Consider this 2000 finding from the University of Wisconsin–Milwaukee School of Social Welfare: One third of 2,375 Milwaukee students said violence in a dating relationship might be deserved if a girl yelled at her boyfriend or insulted him in front of friends. Twenty-three percent said okay to violence if a girl was seen talking to another boy. If a girl hit a boy first, 67 percent thought that violence was an appropriate comeback. If a girl refused to listen to her boyfriend or do what he wanted, 17 percent believed that violence would be the consequence of disobedience.

Obviously, young adolescents—girls, but boys as well—need to identify the difference between appropriate, loving behavior and inappropriate, abusive misbehavior. The confusion for this generation of females stems in part from the toxic experiences and messages they had within girl-to-girl friendships. And what they saw happen.

Read down the following list of typical manhandling misbehaviors and consider how these can appear to be an extension of a girl's earlier susceptibility or brainwashing.

A boyfriend is abusive when . . .

**He monopolizes a girl's time and schedule,** cutting her off from friends and family. He can use the cell phone or the IM function of the computer or a pager to track her. He wants her all to himself.

*Sounds a lot like the old possessive "If you are my friend you can't be her friend," doesn't it?*

**He makes derogatory comments.** Even though he may be sweet and complimentary at first, he soon criticizes her clothing or her personality. Specifically, he focuses on her friendly behavior toward others, which he calls flirting. He turns into the fashion police. Her way of dressing is suddenly slutty. The boy alternates these cuts with pledges of undying love. He loves her so much, he croons, that's why he's so paranoid and jealous.

*This flip-flop from ardent to accusatory is confusing. Girls already know that intimacy can be confusing from when their best girlfriends dissed them, often following an insult with a "Just kidding" or "You know I didn't mean that."*

**He triggers her fear.** The romantic euphoria she felt at first becomes colored with fear. She becomes edgy (perhaps her grades slip or her weight drops or balloons), because she never knows when he'll turn on her.

*Middle school girlfriends are well-versed in trepidation. Many a girl fears the wrong remark, outfit, look, or conversation will bring on social excommunication from her clique. Walking on eggshells is the tweenage gait.*

**His abusive behavior attracts attention.** Others see her being cursed out or intimidated, being pushed or even hit. They tell a parent or teacher about it.

*Girls wince at the sight of a victim being scapegoated or shunned. She may be a friend or a classmate. Yet they are not likely to report this to an adult. They are likely to remember the incident.*

**He is explosive and yet blames her for their fights.** She believes she's at fault.

*Resembles how many a girl feels in her clique dramas, right? Tweenage girls are no strangers to this I'm-not-guilty speech. Powerful divas manipulate, stir the rumor pot, or decide who's in or out, and then act innocent. Many are experts at how to orchestrate dirty tricks and double dealings. The villains act blameless. Somehow the victims wind up feeling at fault.*

Are you getting the drift here? Abusive relationships happen when girls are confused and don't recognize misbehavior, and are anxious to please.

We are not saying that all girls who are exposed to cliques and hurtful episodes within female friendships are destined for romantic disasters. Nor are we saying all boys think along abusive lines. That said, with dating violence statistics on the rise, parents need to be vigilant. Could your daughter be susceptible?

## Watch Out for Abusive Romances

A seventeen-year-old Philadelphia girl (to protect her privacy we'll call her Joanne) fell for a handsome, athletic, popular basketball player because, as she explained, he made her laugh, took her dancing, and wrote her beautiful letters. Then he started acting differently: "I was really confused. I didn't know what to do. He totally degraded me. He was always telling me that I'm fat, I'm a slut, I'm not good enough, and no other guy would love me. I'm lucky to have him."

Rather than ditch the creep, Joanne confessed she wound up fighting with her parents, ignoring her friends, and doing poorly in school.

Being entwined romantically with a creep entails the very same debilitating tactics—guilt, intimidation, isolation, humiliation, and disrespect—that can pollute early girlfriend relationships. Coercion and even physical abuse can follow emotional whiplashing.

A girl like Joanne reacts with that old powerlessness that dogs tweens. Abused girls tend to keep the sad and shameful situation a secret or make excuses. On some level they recognize that there's something wrong with their relationship, but they can't get out. A victim's inertia often becomes an impasse, a hurdle mixed up with confusion, guilt, melodrama, and low self-esteem.

If a parent suspects that a daughter is involved with an abusive creep, she should:

- Act upon her suspicions.
- Talk to her daughter's friends, teachers, and siblings too. Sisters and brothers may know more than you think. Suggest that everyone advise her how unhealthy this romance is and that it is not good for her.
- Approach your daughter delicately. It's not as easy as just forbidding her to continue dating this particular brute. "You can't see him anymore" edicts can turn him into a tragic Romeo figure.
- Learn more about the magnetic pull of a boy who is equal parts adoring and abusing from *Saving Beauty from the Beast* by Vicki Crompton and Ellen Zella Kessner. Coauthor Crompton's daughter was murdered by her boyfriend. This tragedy turned her into an advocate and expert on controlling behavior and teen dating violence.
- Offer to accompany your daughter and her friends to a program on teen dating. Many communities have programs highlighting the complex epidemic of dating abuse.

## Undo the Toxic Messages

The intense and complicated friendships that young adolescent girls revel in (and on occasion revile) deliver positive and negative legacies. How can we ensure our girls take beneficial experiences and lessons with them into their future romances and leave behind any scars? Girls need adult guidance so that they can construct healthy blueprints for future relationships.

Start by talking with your daughter about her friendships. Do her friends and her friendships make her feel good or bad? Emphasize what's valuable in a friendship and how that translates into good romantic relationships.

### Teach Her That Goodwill and Good Wishes Are the Heart of Friendship

Sometimes friends let you down. That's human nature. On occasion, envy and jealousy rear their ugly green heads in friendships between the nicest of folks. But among true friends, there is plenty of rooting for one another and sharing good news. Friends want what is best for one another—that lucky streak, acing that final, being elected class president. They are happy for you when you fall in love and he loves you back. They delight in your successes.

In fact, according to a new set of studies, being able to share kudos plays a significant role in marriage satisfaction. Shelly Gable, an assistant professor of psychology at the University of California at Los Angeles, analyzed how couples shared everyday positive events. In one study, Gamble measured assorted reactions to a job promotion ranging from enthusiastic ("That's wonderful," followed by why you deserved the achievement) to a tepid reaction ("Hmmm that's nice," followed by the mate changing the subject) to a negatively tinged response ("I suppose that's good, but it wasn't much of a raise"). The only correct reaction, according to the research, is the first and most eager affirmation. Basking in and enjoying good fortune together no matter which half of the couple brings in the bonus correlated to intimacy, satisfaction, trust, and commitment. This joined and enjoined sense of joy increased a couple's happiness whether the couple was married or dating.

On the flip side, when good news gets a tepid or passive response, the partner feels immediately less positive, as if the wind has been taken out of his or her sails. The price of this inability to share good tidings is that the purveyor of the news feels less intimacy toward the withholding partner.

Explore with your daughter how her friends react when good things happen. Are they glad or envious? Young adolescent girls easily can grasp this concept. All around girls see peers competing for grades, for popularity, for teachers' attention, for honors small and large, as well as for the affections and attentions of one another. They have a finely tuned feminine sense of knowing when a friend withholds this elusive goodwill. Make certain your daughter practices goodwill toward her friends. If and when envy strikes, help her work through it.

### Listen, Do You Want to Know a Secret?

Distinguish between privacy and secrecy. If you suspect that your child doesn't tell you everything that happens to her in and out of school, your intuition is correct. Remember, young adolescents value their private life. They hide foibles or their own risky forays. Furthermore, they protect their friends. And so your child may not tell you if a friend does something wrong. If you continue to question, she may evade you and chide you for giving her the third degree.

Withholding information from you about a failed test is one thing. But middle schoolers are apt to keep dangerous secrets about themselves or a friend's behavior. They may stay mum if someone embarrasses or bullies them. They may not report to you when they witness an abusive behavior because everyone hates a tattletale.

At this age girls need clarification when it comes to the difference between privacy and secrecy. Reassure your child that you understand her desire to maintain private knowledge with regard to her friends and classmates. Afford your child the privacy that she craves. Knock before you enter her bedroom. Honor her need for modesty and don't barge into the bathroom when she's changing or into the department store dressing room before she's ready to show you how the dress fits. Be discreet with the confidences she shares. Don't snoop.

Distinguish between keeping a confidence and keeping a secret that endangers. Discuss tattling, a concept to which all young adolescents are sensitive. Our children see a lot going on, from cheating on tests to episodes of bullying at the bus stop. They might know a girl has an eating disorder, a boy is juicing steroids, or that another is contemplating cutting herself or worse. Establish that telling an adult something confidential is not "tattling" whenever someone's well-being is at risk. A secret that may bring shame with it—common where any kind of abuse exists—is exactly the type that needs to be told.

When you strip away any misguided loyalty surrounding secrets, you protect your girls from being locked into shameful and sabotaging episodes and relationships.

### Emphasize That Fear Never Belongs in the Same Category as Caring

Tell her over and over: The hallmark of an unhealthy relationship is always and forever fear. Discuss how fear affects her social group. Take a decision such as: Should she go along with Brie and uninvite Anna to a sleepover? Check her if you see that she's behaving like an intimidating diva. How is fear used and against whom? Ask her: Is Brie popular because girls are afraid of her? And then probe: What should make someone popular?

Explore how fear may figure into situations. For example, when hanging with a risk-driven crowd—should she go along and does she take that cigarette or beer to avoid being called a chicken? Is it fear that makes a girl stay with a boy who tries to control things? Make sure your child knows how to identify fear in its subtlest forms, an uneasy self-doubt or a queasy sensation of self-conscious worry.

## Communication—Don't Give Up When the Going Gets Rough

Critiquing prickly adolescents, criticizing their friends—even justifiably—can be difficult. Their backs go up and they tend to brush us off along with our precious instructions. They clam up, withdraw, lash out, and reject us during conversations launched at critical moments. So when it comes to the task of getting points across to your daughter about an issue as incendiary as her friends and the caliber of her friendships, be prepared for conversational failures.

"More tension arises between an adolescent daughter and her mother than between any other parent/child pair," says Terri Apter, PhD, social psychologist and author of a guide to understanding girls titled *You Don't Really Know Me: Why Mothers and Daughters Fight and How Both Can Win*. In her studies of mother-daughter communication ranging over two decades, she found that a conflict erupts on average every two and a half days. In contrast, mothers and adolescent sons quarrel or argue every four days. Most tiffs with a girl are short-lived, lasting about fifteen minutes. Quarrelsome moments with sons are even shorter, and last approximately six minutes.

The drama of intense emotions, arguments, or a breakdown of rapport goes along with early adolescent territory, hormones, and change. There will be times when your daughters can't wait to dish with you about rivals and best girlfriends; there will be other times when they refuse to acknowledge your concern or listen to any advice. Be patient.

It may take years of conversation to undo the damage of girls' weakness and meanness to one another. Rest assured that the push and pull of your rapport about divas and creeps, good love and bad, healthy friendships and unhealthy misbehaviors will affect your daughter. Your influence and involvement can eat away at the social and romantic handicaps, the result of the middle school mean machine, that will inevitably crop up.

Never underestimate the influence of your maternal words. A 2001 *Journal of Research on Adolescence* study found that asking questions about a child's friends, activities, and schoolwork paid off. Parents who monitored their children through conversations wound up with kids who drank less often, delayed sexual activity, and experienced less depression. So even though she may rant and pout, cry and disagree loudly, she still takes everything you say up to her room where she will mull it over. Apter insists that the vast majority of young people "like their parents, share their values, and seek a good relationship." Your rapport can make your daughter a kinder, better friend. It can change the way she sees her friendships and raise the bar on the expectations she holds for her girlfriends . . . and future romantic partners.

But these are merely starting points that will lead to the two of you weighing other significant questions: What role does your daughter play in her social world—a passive one or an active leading role? What is she willing to sacrifice in the name of friendship—her good name, her conscience, other girls, her grades, her desires?

Helping your daughter make sense of her platonic relationships with other girls is the key to preparing her for happy and well-adjusted expectations about caring, nurturing, and later romantic love. Even though you may often feel powerless to help a hurting daughter, you do hold the secret to the ultimate girl power in your hands.

# CHAPTER 5

# I Want to Hold Your Hand

## *The Ins and Outs of Dating*

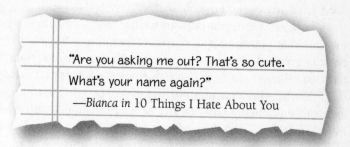

> "Are you asking me out? That's so cute.
> What's your name again?"
> —*Bianca in* 10 Things I Hate About You

"I remember my first date as if it were yesterday," says one mother. "His name was John and we went to an amusement park with a youth group from the YMCA." As she recalls, the day was filled with cotton candy, arcade games, rides on the Ferris wheel and Tilt-A-Whirl, and a little handholding. "He knocked down milk bottles with a ball and won me a pink teddy bear," she says, laughing. "We had a great time."

The next week, it was back to the rigors of seventh-grade math and social studies. "He never asked me out again," she says. "That was okay with me. We had a good time, but I liked him better as a friend."

Still, she enjoyed the formality of the date—being asked, accepting, deciding what to wear, being picked up, enduring the embarrassment of parental scrutiny, and anticipating the goodnight kiss. (In this case, a peck on the cheek.)

"Sometimes I feel sad that my daughter is missing out on that experience," she confesses. "Yet, when I hear about kids hooking up on dates, I am secretly happy she's not dating."

Ambivalence about dating runs rampant among parents these days. Many look back with nostalgia upon their own dating experiences. Yet in the current youth culture, they worry that a dream date could very well turn into a nightmare. "I'm scared to death of my daughter dating," one mother says. "I don't trust any of the boys these days."

Once upon a time, dating—in archaic terms, courting—was the way that young people prepared themselves for marriage. Back in colonial days (and even among some cultures today), parents arranged for their children to meet under strict conditions. During these encounters, the young people got to know each other gradually without any pressure to engage in sexual intimacy. In fact, aside from a hug or chaste kiss, physical contact was nearly impossible, owing to the watchful eye of more than one parent or adult.

By the mid-twentieth century, parents no longer played the role of matchmaker. The dating ritual was the primary vehicle for meeting and getting to know someone else. As the mother above recalled, children as young as seventh-graders went on dates. These pairings often involved adult-supervised outings with an organization like the Y, boys and girls clubs, a church or school group. Basketball games, school dances, or even sharing a soda at the local malt shop were other ways kids spent time together. These fifties dates smacked of innocence and awkwardness. Parents and adolescents alike saw it as a process, a way of learning about relationships. Fathers schooled their sons on chivalry—pulling out the girl's chair, opening a car door, presenting her with a corsage. Mothers encouraged their daughters to dream about romance, finding that perfect someone who would treat them with kindness and respect.

These days those stereotypical roles seem outdated and sexist. Young women no longer wait by the phone for a Saturday night date. Instead they go out with a group of girls, or with a group of boys and girls, which removes the stigma of being dateless while allowing the freedom to meet and socialize with a larger number of people.

So what's wrong with that? Indeed, many of the parents we talked with in our focus groups not only approved of but also encouraged the concept of group dating. "There's safety in numbers," was the belief we heard stated over and over again. Having a daughter go on a date solo was tantamount to endorsing sexual activity.

Are parents overreacting? Should all one-on-one dating among young adolescents be discouraged? Is socializing in groups a safer way to go? And if parents can't forbid dating forever, how can they tell when their daughter is ready, truly ready, to date?

How has dating changed in just the short time since today's parents were young adolescents? There are new rules, as well as new language to describe the social scene as our children view it. We will explore the pros and cons of one-on-one dating, as well as group dating. Neither is as dangerous or as safe as parents think. We will give guidelines on how to educate and protect your daughter, whether she flies solo or with her friends.

How can a father help his daughter understand, evaluate, and appreciate the boys she meets? A father is the first man in his daughter's life, the first male figure that she uses to compare and contrast with others she meets. What can a father do to make sure his daughter views him as the role model he hopes to be?

Mothers have great influence, of course. Daughters identify with their mothers and in the best-case scenario hope to emulate them. Actions often speak just as loudly as words. Mothers who operate as equals with their partners empower their daughters to make wise choices.

By the end of this chapter, you will have a better understanding of how adolescents socialize and how you can influence your daughter so that her interactions are safe, educational, and fun.

## Dating, Then and Now

No one has to tell you that the dating scene has changed dramatically since you were a teenager. "Dating seems a lot more casual," says one high school girl. "Guys don't ever pick you up. And boys hang out with girls who are just friends."

Let's take the one major date experience that most of us remember—the prom. Chances are you can remember your date, what you wore, if he brought you an orchid corsage, which best friend you doubled with, who snared the king and queen crowns, what you did afterward, and what time you came home. Your memories may be happy ones or filled with angst, if your date turned out to be more a nightmare than a dream. Perhaps you skipped the prom because you didn't have a date and instead spent the night watching TV with other date-challenged friends.

Couples ruled. The prom was the big event a girl couldn't go to unless she had a date. That often meant waiting for that all-important phone call from a boy.

Fast-forward to the new millennium. Now both boys and girls go "stag," that is, dateless, to proms and other special events. Many applaud the new rule because it removes the stigma of not having someone to go with and allows girls to be themselves and have a good time without relying on a boy. "Last year, so many seniors went stag to the winter dance," says one fifteen-year-old. "You can have as much fun without a date."

While girls feel less stigmatized going alone, parents endorse the dateless prom because they feel it is safer. Without an actual date, parents feel, girls have less opportunity to engage in sexual activity.

Talking to the kids, however, a different picture emerges. Even though a girl may go to the prom dateless, once there she can easily pair up with a boy who comes stag. What is lost in the process is the entire routine of going as a couple to this special event. Parents, needless to say, never have the chance to meet the boy their daughter may spend the evening with.

Being able to go stag to the prom is only one visible change on the dating scene. Here are some others:

**Group dating is widespread and acceptable.** Both parents and kids endorse this method for socializing though there are both benefits and dangers. (More on this issue later.)

**The quantity of special events for middle schoolers has increased.** In times past, attending a fancy dress-up dance was the privilege of being in high school. Now, many kids are jaded by the time they reach the junior and senior proms. Middle school students are seasoned partygoers. Holiday and moving-up dances, bar and bat mitzvahs, and elaborate birthday parties at upscale restaurants jam a young girl's calendar.

**After-prom parties may include coed sleepovers.** Safety issues convinced many parents to agree to the previously unthinkable—boys and girls together at a slumber party. Rather than having teens driving, after possibly drinking, the all-night party in someone's home was supposed to give parents peace of mind. Yet some parents feel this solution presented other problems. Hosting parents many times do not supervise closely. "I found out that kids were having sex at the coed sleepover," one mother says. "When I told my daughter, her response was, 'Well, I didn't, so what are you worried about?' "

**Kids don't say "going steady."** The proper phrase is "going out with." If your daughter has a date, she will probably tell you she is "talking" with a boy. It's okay to go out with another person while still in the talking stage with another. If a girl is "going out with" a boy, however, that relationship would be exclusive.

**"Hooking up" doesn't involve installing a telephone.** The term is used to describe any number of sexual encounters. With middle schoolers hooking up usually means what we used to call "making out" or "necking." With older adolescents, hooking up may mean going further, having oral sex or possibly intercourse.

**Kids rarely exchange class rings.** Remember when "going steady" meant the boy and girl traded class rings? She would wind tape around his to make it fit, while he would wear hers on his pinky. In today's materialistic society, tokens of affection are more apt to be pieces of jewelry or other items (perfume, purses, electronic devices) that are more expensive and sophisticated.

**Public displays of affection (PDAs) are in.** Physical intimacy is no longer reserved for a private moment. More than one couple has been found in the school hallways pawing and groping each other between classes.

**Forget the waltz.** Dirty dancing is the order of the day, with even middle schoolers bumping and grinding on the dance floor. Also popular—the sandwich, where two boys envelop a girl, dancing as close to her as possible.

**Drugs are readily available.** "Every single party you go to, there are drugs—marijuana, cocaine, LSD, Esctasy, mushrooms," says one high school girl. While the harder drugs, like heroine and crack, may be used by the high school crowd, middle schoolers are at risk of being exposed to marijuana. The latest threat, prescription drugs and over-the-counter cold remedies and cough syrups—available in every parent's medicine cabinet—are being abused by ten- to fifteen-year-olds.

**Girls may have boys who are just friends and nothing more.** "My parents believe you can't have a platonic relationship with a boy," says one girl. "My mother thinks of what could happen and becomes anxious."

**Some friendships, however, do become sexual.** "Friends with benefits" means that a boy and girl are basically friends, but may engage in sexual activity now and then without committing to a serious one-on-one relationship. This arrangement, once popular in high school and college, has been cropping up among younger teens.

Many young people embrace the casual approach to the dating scene, including everything from group dating to friends with benefits. Even young adolescents feel intense pressure to get good grades, play a variety of sports, and excel on the stage. Why, they believe, should they add the pressure to find a date for Saturday night? Far easier to stick with a group or hang with guy friends. A girl who develops that pattern in middle school and high school may find it difficult to break the pattern after graduation.

What she loses, however, is the opportunity to develop her social skills, one-on-one. Ultimately, both boys and girls will think about marriage and family. Yet their early years do not provide them with any sort of a road map for arriving at that destination. "Today, there are no socially prescribed forms of conduct that help guide young men and women in the direction of marriage," says Dr. Leon R. Kass, chairman of the President's Council on Bioethics. In his paper "The End of Courtship," Kass notes that the growing number of failed marriages may be partially attributable to the absence of courtship customs. And while most young men and women would argue that marriage is not and should not be their top priority early on, being able to maintain a relationship with another person probably is something they think about a lot and spend a lot of energy on.

Learning about relationships, however, should not be just a

college-level course. One high school counselor said that the young people she meets crave commitment, but because they have avoided dating when younger, they feel ill-equipped to pursue relationships. Some interaction needs to happen earlier. Parents can help, not by panicking, but by learning about their daughter's social scene and finding positive ways to influence and intervene.

## Friends and Lovers—
## Separate or Equal?

One of the most distinct changes in adolescent relationships has to do with friends. To most parents, the term *boyfriend* describes a boy who is more than a friend, that is, someone a daughter is romantically involved with. Girls these days are as likely to spend time with boys who are just friends, and nothing more. In some cases, a girl may have a boy who is a best friend, someone she depends on and confides in. "Guy friends can be helpful," says one girl.

Will such a close bond evolve into something more? Sometimes, but often not. The girls we talked with in focus groups told us that boys who are friends rarely turn into bona-fide boyfriends. "I wouldn't date a boy I was friends with," says one girl from Virginia.

In fact, a 2002 study from Ohio State University found that girls who had mostly male friends were less likely to have sex by the time they were sixteen. "This may seem counterintuitive until you consider that preteen girls who hang out mostly with boys may be the more active, sports-oriented girls traditionally called tomboys," says Elizabeth Cooksey, a study coauthor and an associate professor of sociology at Ohio State University.

"My daughter is living a real-life *Friends*," says one mother, referring to the popular show where three men and women form fast friendships. Young adolescents can have platonic friends of the opposite sex. Group dating has promoted the idea that girls and boys can go out together without being romantically involved. In some ways, what's happening among adolescents echoes what is happening in the workplace. As women seek to gain a stronger foothold in corporations, they must work side by side with men and remain platonic in order to succeed professionally.

Of course, no one can forget that office romances do happen. And, in fact, the taboo that used to forbid it has dissolved when both parties are eligible. Even on *Friends,* four of the group ended up as couples. Some sexual tension will always exist when a boy and girl are close, particularly when they share their most intimate thoughts and secrets.

Some people do not think it's necessarily bad that a relationship that begins as a friendship evolves into something more. One father says when his son was having trouble deciding who to ask to the prom, he suggested a certain girl. "He told me, 'Oh, Dad, she's just a friend,' " the father recalled, laughing. "I reminded him that I had married my best friend, his mother."

The friendships your daughter has, whether with girls or boys, can be a good starting point for discussing relationships. Listen to one girl describe what she looks for in a boyfriend: "Respect, personality. The way he treats himself and others. The way he acts around his parents and friends. Whether he is disrespectful. He can't lie. I can't stand liars."

These characteristics are also those that make for a good friend. In a true friendship, trust is paramount. How else to be sure that your friend will keep your secrets, give you the best advice? Anyone who has had a falling out with a good friend knows that this breakup can be as traumatic or more so as the end of a love affair. Friendships, like romantic relationships, require intimacy. Drawing closer to someone else can feel both comforting and scary. If your daughter gives more than she receives from a friendship, she may feel manipulated and may choose to end the relationship. The same should hold in a romantic relationship. And you can make that point when the time comes.

## A Time for Every Social Season

You probably don't want to keep your social butterfly in a cocoon her whole life. You know she is eager to spread her wings and fly. Your challenge is to oversee her coming out in a safe and timely manner. How do you manage that? By paying attention to the ages and stages of her social development, gauging when she is ready to move on from all-girl groups to mixed sex gatherings, and, finally, a one-on-one date with a boy.

Parents frequently ask us what social situations are appropriate for young adolescents. To a great extent, it depends on the individual child. One parent described her fourteen-year-old daughter as a mini Pearl Mesta, the Washington socialite noted for bringing famous people together. "That's my daughter's persona," the mother says with a sigh. "She's always arranging parties and outings and I'm always fielding calls from concerned parents wondering what's going on." Another father complained about his thirteen-year-old daughter being a social recluse. "I'm glad she hasn't discovered boys yet, because it makes my life easier. But, at the same time, I wonder, is there something wrong with her?"

When it comes to encouraging your daughter's social development, there are no easy answers. The best strategy is to work with your daughter and take your cues from her. Although there is no set age for sticking with girls, going out in mixed groups, or dating, we can make generalizations based on what parents and the girls themselves have told us. We stress that these ages and stages, as laid out in chapter 2, are flexible and totally dependent upon the maturity of your own child. Still, the guidance we offer for each type of social gathering will help you figure out what precautions you should take along the way.

### Only Girls Allowed

All-girl gatherings at home make up the first rung on your daughter's social ladder. In grade school, you arrange play dates at your house, coordinating with friends' parents. Once your daughter is in middle school, these same-sex social events take on added importance. Friends are a significant part of a young adolescent's life. Learning how to make and keep friends is a life skill. When your daughter makes decisions about friends, what she likes about them, what she receives from the relationship, she stores up valuable information that will serve as a baseline for choosing her companions in the future. Her encounters with girls lay the groundwork for her interactions with boys. So you want her to have plenty of positive interaction with her friends.

At this time you should encourage your daughter to host get-togethers in your home. These festivities can range from birthday celebrations to sleepovers to pizza parties. She may invite two or twenty-two of her closest friends. Don't leave her to handle all the arrangements, however. Young adolescents often fall short when it comes to nailing down details. Your opinion and guidance can prevent many a disaster. Where there are friends, there are cliques. Make sure the guest list (particularly if it grows to more than half the girls in your daughter's class) is inclusive and no one is being purposely left out. (One mother told us her daughter was sent a noninvitation to a party telling her to stay away.) Keep yourself in the loop.

Tell other parents you will be present during the party. Help your daughter plan any formal activity that might happen. If the girls want to watch a movie, make sure no one will be offended by the choice.

While helping your daughter be the hostess is exhausting, you will be rewarded tenfold. You are the "fly on the wall," passing out the chips and dip, remaining low key, yet coming away with a true understanding of your daughter and her friends.

## All Around the Town

"A new Disney movie had just come out and my daughter said she wanted to see it with her friends," one mother told us. " 'Great!' I told her. 'I'll get the tickets and we can meet Jessie and Nicole at the theater.' " However, having her mother tag along was the last thing this twelve-year-old wanted. "Mom," she said, rolling her eyes, "we want to go by ourselves. You can pick us up."

This mother worried about more than missing the latest Disney flick. Would her daughter be safe by herself in a dark movie theater? Do sexual predators come to kid flicks, hoping to target an unsuspecting girl? Could she be assaulted in the bathroom? Suddenly, the mother's thoughts were revolving less around Nemo and more around *Psycho*. Was this all-girl outing a ruse? Would *Toy Story* morph into *Love Story*?

Yet she could understand her daughter's desire for more independence. Rather than veto the idea, she called the other parents and worked out a plan. They selected an afternoon movie to eliminate having the girls out after dark. One of the mothers would drop the girls off, a father would later pick them up. The girls were instructed to stay together, particularly if they visited a rest room. One of the girls kept her cell phone handy so that she could call or text-message in the event of trouble. Nicole's parents promised to be at home and available.

The only concession the parents made was arranging to pick the girls up a block from the theater, rather than in the lobby. "Mom," the twelve-year-old pleaded, "we'll look like dorks if someone sees us being picked up by Nicole's dad."

Letting go is difficult, some might even say terrifying, for parents. (Parents have confessed to secretly following their young adolescents just to ease their fears.) The world our children are growing up in is much more dangerous and unpredictable than anything we knew. Concerns are not unwarranted. Still, these girls, right on schedule, pushed to be on their own, away from the watchful eye of parents. With careful parental involvement, such outings are an important next step on the social ladder.

## Where the Boys Are

All-girl get-togethers will always be important to your daughter, whether she's thirteen or thirty. Around age thirteen or fourteen, however, she will push to be with the boys. Some of these encounters will be spontaneous, casual, and safe, sitting with boys at a school basketball game, for example. When there is no set activity where your daughter can meet boys, however, the alternative may be less to your liking.

"When my daughter hit thirteen, she longed to be with the boys," one mother recalled. Middlers, being notoriously disorganized, rarely come up with a realistic plan for a social activity where boys and girls can be together. This mother discovered that her daughter's idea of meeting boys was to wander around her city's downtown area, hoping the right boys would show up. Obviously, this plan was not going to fly.

At thirteen, this mother felt her daughter was too young to date, but she understood her daughter's desire to be with boys. So she worked with her daughter to create a safe environment where a group could enjoy one another's company and the parents involved would feel reassured that the event was being properly chaperoned. She opened her home to the young people, allowing her daughter to invite over a small group to watch a movie.

Sooner or later, however, young adolescents resist having parents hover over them. Parents often panic when this happens, assuming the worst—that sexual activity is around the corner. More than likely, however, middlers, still finding their way socially, are often embarrassed to be so closely scrutinized by their parents. An outside event, such as going to a movie, ball game, amusement park, or other event, can be a perfect opportunity for them to try out their independence. Parents can take the responsibility for dropping off and picking up.

Make sure, however, that if the group comes up with a plan, it sticks with it. Groups have a way of splintering off into smaller clusters or even couples. Your daughter should know that you expect her to follow the schedule you approved. If there is any deviation, she should call you and ask for permission to make that change.

Peer pressure may come into play, making it hard for your daughter to say no to her friends. "Groups don't always keep you safe," one girl says. One safeguard, she adds, is to always have a curfew and make sure friends know what it is. Role-play with your daughter to give her some strategies for opting out while saving face. She should feel free to blame you, the parent, for not letting her venture into a certain club or stay out past a certain hour. Next time, perhaps, she may decide hanging with this group is not worth her time and trouble.

## Three's a Crowd

You know what comes next—the one-on-one date. When your instincts tell you your daughter is mature enough to handle being alone with a boy (more on that later), you can once again help ease her transition. Encourage her to invite the boy over. Promise her some alone time, yet make sure they both know you are around and will be checking in occasionally.

Adolescent romances oftentimes have a brief shelf life. You may find yourself playing host to more than one boy over the course of a few months. That's okay, too. Your daughter is getting to know different boys, and you are in the catbird seat of meeting them. Try not to criticize her choices, but make observations along the way that might get your daughter thinking about her preferences.

Finally, your daughter will progress to the one-on-one date outside your home. At one talk we gave, a concerned father pleaded with us to endorse his opinion that his fifteen-year-old daughter was too young to go to a movie with a boy. We empathized with his fear, picturing his innocent daughter in a dark movie theater with a boy after "just one thing." Yet his solution, opting for her going to the movies with a group, was not necessarily better. She might still pair off with the boy, and the father would have missed the opportunity to create boundaries that would keep his daughter safe. In a group, there may be pressure to "hook up" before she is ready for such physical contact.

Don't make that mistake. The better strategy is to encourage your daughter to invite the boy over beforehand so that you can meet him and go over your expectations. Get a rundown of the evening's event. If they plan to see a movie, has he already bought the tickets? If not, offer to do so online. Where will they go after the movie? Make sure the boy knows your daughter's curfew. If needed, volunteer to pick them up.

Adolescents are known for deviating from the evening's agenda at the drop of a hat. "Oh, the movie was sold out, so we spent the evening walking in the park." Never mind that the park is a haven for panhandlers and drug dealers. Reinforce the point that they must make a plan and stick to it. Ask to be called if there are any changes so that you know where they are and when your daughter will be home.

"My fifteen-year-old daughter went on her first date a week ago and I felt panicked," one mother says. "It reminded me of when she would go on the scariest ride." Fortunately, this girl's date didn't drive and so the girl's parents volunteered to drop them off and pick them up. "Since the boy was too young to drive, we felt we could still control the situation," says the mother.

Even before the big event, however, the girl's parents invited the boy over to dinner. His father came to drive him home. Together, the families worked out some ground rules. "His father said he didn't want them in our basement alone. Neither did we! So we knew we were on the same page," the mother said.

As it turned out, the boy's mother ended up driving them to the movies, and the girl's parents drove them home. The girl's mother doesn't regret being so strict. "Right now, I'll set the boundaries. Later on, she can set her own boundaries," she says.

## TIMETABLE

| Social Group | Location | Ages | Benefits | Risks | Parental Involvement |
|---|---|---|---|---|---|
| All girls | Your home | All ages | Bonding, practice friendship skills | Clique-forming, possible drinking and/or drug use if not well supervised | Supervise guest list, buy food, check in from time to time |
| All girls | Outside | 12 and up | Bonding, independence building | May meet girls or boys not in the group, possible alcohol and/or drug use, possible pairing off to "hook up" | Supervise arrangements, drop off and pick up |
| Girls/boys | Your home | 13 and up | Practice social skills in a safe environment | Clandestine use of alcohol and/or drugs, sneaking off to other rooms to "hook up" | Supervise guest list, talk to other parents, be on-site, rule certain rooms off-limits |
| Girls/boys | Outside | 14 and up | Socialize with boys without pressure to land a date | Possible pairing off to "hook up," alcohol and/or drug use | Set boundaries: type of activity, travel plans, curfew |

## TIMETABLE (CONT'D)

| Social Group | Location | Ages | Benefits | Risks | Parental Involvement |
|---|---|---|---|---|---|
| Girl/boy | Your home | 14 and up | Socialize one-on-one in a safe environment, get to meet boy | Possible hooking up, possible alcohol and/or drug use | Set boundaries: which areas of house are off-limits, keep a physical presence |
| Girl/boy | Outside | 14 and up | Experience a real date, evaluate a boy's social skills, parents get to meet boy | Possible hooking up, possible alcohol and/or drug use | Set boundaries: type of activity, transportation, checking in, curfew |

## Casual Dating vs. Going Steady

In Middler World, having a boyfriend or girlfriend puts a young adolescent on the map. "Girls definitely feel it's bad if you don't have a boyfriend," admits one girl. "They will talk about how they have to go manhunting."

Parents are of two minds. Having a steady boyfriend means their daughter will curtail manhunting activities that could lead to trouble. Yet spending time alone with the same boy also presents problems.

"Parents may not like this, but nearly all [teenage] sexual intercourse happens within the context of going steady," says Robin Sawyer, assistant professor of health education at the University of Maryland. "It's when you see an awful lot of someone and you start to feel awfully comfortable with them" that sexual experimentation happens.

Elizabeth Cooksey, of Ohio State University, agrees. "A steady relationship correlates with early sexual behavior, regardless of how often a teenager goes on dates," she says. "So frequent dating—as opposed to going steady—may be more innocuous than going steady when it comes to initiating sexual behavior."

Experts believe that young adolescents should be discouraged from going steady. Here are the pitfalls they have identified.

**Intimacy is mistaken for commitment.** An adolescent girl might mistake intense sexual activity for assurance that she is the boy's one and only love. That vow may be true—today. But when the sexual ardor cools, the boy may move on, leaving the girl hurt, angry, and confused.

**Friends get lost in the shuffle.** While learning about the opposite sex is part of the adolescent experience, so is learning about and keeping friendships. When a couple spends all their time together, they exclude their friends and isolate themselves.

**Schoolwork may suffer.** Being in love, especially when that relationship involves sex, interferes with a young person's focus on academics and planning for a future career. Daydreaming in math class, text messaging each other during study hall, and IMing all night rather than doing homework pushes school and extracurricular activities to the bottom of the heap.

**Breakups can be traumatic.** Few young adolescent romances are long-lasting. And when the breakup comes, heartache usually follows.

**Self-esteem hinges on having a boyfriend.** During the adolescent years, girls need to find their own voice, talents, strengths, and passions. When having a boyfriend becomes the most important goal on the list, other goals may suffer.

**Dates can be expensive.** Although the burden traditionally fell on the guy to finance an evening of fun, increasingly kids are going Dutch or the girl assumes all or part of the tab, particularly if she extends the invitation.

## Mistletoe, Anyone?

If sexual initiation is going to happen, can parents predict when? Sociologists from Mississippi say many teens who are dating seriously choose December as the time to have sex for the first time. Their findings led them to predict that teens with romantic partners are nearly three times more likely to make their sexual debut in December than those dating casually. The researchers credited the increase to all the togetherness surrounding the holidays. "We call it the 'Santa Clause effect,'" says Martin Levin, lead author of the 2002 study, which was published in the *Journal of Marriage and Family*.

The data was drawn from the ongoing National Longitudinal Study of Adolescent Health and the responses of nearly 21,000 teens, as young as seventh-graders. The Mississippi researchers cross-referenced the month teens say they lost their virginity with responses to questions about the seriousness of their relationships with sexual partners.

Still, June remains the most common month for teens in general to have sex for the first time.

One warning sign is a child having more friends in higher grades. "Watch out for older guys," one sixteen-year-old told us. "They don't always have a positive influence on younger girls."

## Old Enough to Date?

Your daughter may be telling you she is old enough to go on a one-on-one date. Her classmates may be dating. She knows boys and is comfortable talking with them. Is that enough? Other factors come into play. You need to assess your own child's readiness. Some children can mature faster than others, so evaluate how your daughter measures up. Here are some guidelines:

- She has friends of both sexes and these relationships are healthy and based on shared common interests, rather than who is cool and popular.
- She treats her peers with respect and demands the same in return.
- She shows responsibility in how she manages other aspects of her life, her schoolwork, sports, money, and family.
- She consistently honors her curfews and tells you what she will be doing, when, where, and with whom.
- She has no objection when you ask to meet her date before she goes out with him.

## Home Alone

While some parents worry about their daughters dating, other mothers and fathers are faced with the opposite problem. Their daughters are the proverbial wallflowers, never being asked to dance, ignored by the boys, spending many a Saturday evening in their bedrooms while their girlfriends go out. While the other girls giggle and trade stories about their blossoming love affairs, these passed-over girls suffer from being overlooked.

Of course, all parents believe their daughter is the most beautiful, charming, and engaging girl alive. What boy wouldn't die to date her? The fact that this girl attracts no attention from the opposite sex brings out the protective lioness in many a mother. "You're too smart for these dumb guys." "They're just after one thing, and they know you won't give it to them." "You're beautiful and someday you'll find the perfect boy who will recognize that beauty."

These comments, while well intentioned, may not do the trick. Not only is she embarrassed among her friends, now even her parents feel sorry for her! After all, you are her parents. You have to tell her she's wonderful. Young adolescent girls live in the here and now. One day she may indeed find her one true love, but right now she just wants to be a normal girl, going out with a boy, mooning over him, crying when they break up. Why is this totally normal social life eluding her? Explore these:

**She's small and young-looking.** Even though your daughter is fifteen, she may look like she's ten. Is it fair that the boys are attracted to the more mature, voluptuous girls in the class? No, but sometimes it happens, and that lack of attention can hurt. Talk to your daughter about what attracts her to a boy and what she hopes a boy will see in her. Get her focused on her strengths, not her weaknesses.

**She's scared.** Even though she wants to date, she may be frightened by what she sees her friends go through. Does she seem uncomfortable when a boy does pay attention to her? What does she think will happen if she returns his attention? Explain that she doesn't have to be alone with a boy she likes. She can have a group over to her house to watch a movie, for example.

**She liked a boy and was rebuffed.** Once burned, twice shy. Help her see that during adolescence, she can count on more misses than hits, but that she shouldn't drop out of the game.

**She may be confused about her sexuality.** Some girls hit puberty later than others. Your daughter may still be at the stage where she prefers the company of girls to boys. Does this mean she may be gay? Not necessarily. (For more information, read chapter 9.) She may, however, be worried about her sexuality. Keep the lines of communication open so that she will come to you when she is ready to talk.

## Like Mother, Like Daughter

A new twist these days is that daughters are watching their mothers date. "My parents were divorced when I was two," one high school girl told us. "She's not religious; I am." These mother-daughter discussions often turn into role reversal, with the daughter taking the more conservative viewpoint.

Another high school girl says she and her single mom frequently talk about their boyfriends. "We vent to each other," she says. Some of her mother's friends don't approve of their relationship, which operates more on a peer level than parent-child. But she says her mother's openness helps her evaluate her own relationships.

One thing most girls we talked to were in agreement about: they wanted to hear more about their mother's dating experiences; what worked and what didn't. "My parents married right out of college," one girl says. "They discovered too late that they are too different. My dad is New Age, while my mother is a high-powered executive." In this case, the old adage "opposites attract" proved untrue.

Michael Gurian, in his book, *The Wonder of Girls,* advises a mother to ask her daughter, "If I were going to do things differently with your dad, do you want to know what they might be?" Initially, he says, a daughter will say no, but eventually curiosity will win out. And the mother will have a prime moment for sharing thoughts and guiding her daughter.

What thoughts might she share? Here are some insights from other mothers:

"I'd tell my daughter that it's okay to compromise. When I was younger and into my radical feminist period, I thought any giving in on my part showed weakness. Now I realize that a good relationship survives because of compromise, whether it's something trivial, like having fish instead of chicken, or something more serious, like moving to another city."

"My parents didn't want me to marry my husband, and, my mother, in particular, was quite rude to him. I never called her on her behavior, hoping things would just get better on their own. The situation did improve eventually, but I would tell my daughter to be more supportive of her husband, even if it means siding with him against me!"

"My advice would be to keep your girlfriends for yourself and make couple friends for both of you. Friends are truly a gift you give to yourself."

"I would tell my daughters to be more independent, not so needy. I should have found some way to pursue my goals and not made them second to our relationship. I would tell them not to lose themselves in someone else."

"I would have spent more time with my husband."

"I would tell my daughter to listen more and talk less."

## Father Knows Best

Appearing on *The Oprah Winfrey Show,* the actress Gwyneth Paltrow told a story about her late father, producer Bruce Paltrow. When she was ten years old, her father took her to Paris for the weekend. After a magical two days staying at the Ritz, eating in fine restaurants, they flew home. He asked her if she knew why they made the trip alone, leaving Gwyneth's mother, Blythe Danner, and brother at home in California. She said no. He told her he wanted her first trip to Paris to be with a man who would always love her.

While few fathers can afford a quick jaunt to Paris, many are following Paltrow's example to set a high standard for the boys and young men who will date their daughters. The *Washington Times* profiled an ex–Prince George's County police officer who took his daughter on a date every week after she turned sixteen. "I strove to be a role model so she would know what a gentleman acts like," he explains.

Another dad in Colorado took his daughter on her first date. Their evening included picking up his daughter, escorting her to the car, opening the car door, checking her seat belt, taking her to a nice restaurant, having a wonderful meal together, paying the bill, leaving a tip, and then escorting her home. He told her at the end of the evening, "Never accept less than what you had tonight."

Besides treating his daughter well, the role model father makes sure to treat the other women in his life with care and respect, whether that woman is his wife, mother, mother-in-law, sister, female coworker, or neighbor. That behavior soon becomes the norm, and when a daughter is with a boy who behaves badly, the contrast will be jarring.

How would husbands answer Gurian's question, telling their daughters what they would have done differently with their wives? Men we talked with told us the following:

> "I would try to be more understanding of my wife's tardiness and disorganization."

> "I would tell my wife once in a while why I want to be better for her, why she inspires me. I don't do that often enough and I want my daughter to expect better."

## The Dating Game

Back in the 1960s, *The Dating Game* was a popular show on TV. A young woman questioned three young men who sat behind a screen. Listening to the men's answers, the woman was able to learn something about them. Finally, she chose to go on a date with the one whose answers met with her approval.

As your daughter navigates adolescence, she is playing a real-life dating game with all the boys she meets. You can help her in this journey by giving her the benefit of your wisdom and experience. Keep her safe by establishing appropriate boundaries. But, at the right times, give her the freedom to learn about relationships through trial and error.

# CHAPTER 6

# You Make Me Feel Like a Natural Woman

*How Love and Romance Work*

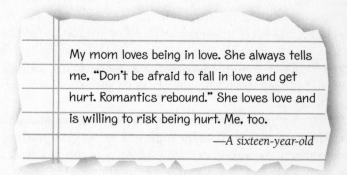

My mom loves being in love. She always tells me, "Don't be afraid to fall in love and get hurt. Romantics rebound." She loves love and is willing to risk being hurt. Me, too.

—*A sixteen-year-old*

Where will I ever find my soul mate?
How will I know when it's the real thing?
Am I the kind of girl a boy can fall in love with?
How can I survive without him?

These are a few of the profound questions that weigh on the minds of countless young adolescent girls. Many are determined to find the answers.

Discovering the right answers to a puzzling social life and the best formulas for romantic success, in all likelihood, will interfere with academic concentration. And so mothers and fathers gauge a daughter's mooning time with concern. They too find themselves beset with questions that usually come down to one: *Will tweenage romantic rapture (or rupture) distract my daughter too much?*

Yes, parents fret that this hormonal fog will cloud a daughter's judgment and, in particular, edge out sensible priorities. By "priorities," most adults mean academic achievements and extracurricular activities that will enhance future opportunities.

A parent's eye looks toward college even when (or even before) children are in middle school. Meanwhile, a young adolescent girl envisions being popular and attractive to boys. Her decisions revolve around assessing what is hot and who is cool, not what is good for college applications. She may want to drop out of marching band, chorus, or mathletes, claiming geeks are not hot. Her game may be off on the soccer field because she's flipping her ponytail or nervously checking out the boys watching from the sidelines. She hears violins, all right, but not the one collecting dust, the one she's supposed to be practicing.

Since her adolescent heart is pumping overtime and since her mind seems fixated on the game of love, why not teach her more about how love works? When a girl is twelve or fourteen, neither popularity nor romance seems simple. The quest to find herself and that elusive "one person" presses on a girl's mind and takes on strains of the impossible dream. (Come to think of it, love may not seem simple to you now, as an adult, either. That's even more likely if your marriage feels strained, or if you are divorced, or remarried.) We hope to shed light on these issues.

Girls are eager to learn all they can about romance. They feel anxious and insecure about whether or not they possess whatever it takes to turn a boy's head and his heart around. We've rounded up information here from psychologists and social scientists who have made many fascinating discoveries about how true love happens and how romantic relationships thrive against the odds. Furthermore, we've collected some worthwhile strategies that will help you console a child when love comes crashing down. By peppering your talks and tactics with this knowledge, you will deliver much reassurance and, in the process, lessen your tweenager's anxiety and angst. If you heed the advice that follows, you can make your daughter feel more like a natural woman than she ever thought possible.

## Is It Time to Open the Book of Love?

Shouldn't you and shouldn't she care more about that algebra and Spanish than about love lessons? No. Once a child enters a reality where managing her schoolwork competes with social butterfly goals, the time has come to introduce the romance training alongside the academic nudging. Getting that love/work/family ratio right turns out to be a lifetime challenge for women (and men), doesn't it? Learning to juggle practical and pragmatic responsibilities with affairs of the heart is a balancing act no matter how old you are. Why not help her get a head start?

It bears repeating that young adolescents are growing physically, emotionally, psychologically, socially, and intellectually. The years between ten and fifteen encompass mastering so many skills and agendas. With a psychic plate so full of change, keeping a child on track academically means competing with other equally valid needs.

Take a moment to get an idea of how school goes for many tweens. During the course of middle school, nearly all young adolescents hit the wall academically speaking. Girls and boys, including honor roll scholars and borderline students, are susceptible to distractions, underachievement, and even failure. A variety of factors lie beneath poor performance.

Let us remind you that the brain grows and plateaus between the ages of ten to fourteen. Each brain adheres to a unique schedule. That means that in a typical seventh-grade classroom, some students comprehend sophisticated concepts in mathematics or analytical themes in literature while others are physiologically unable to grasp the same material.

As if brains playing tricks isn't stressful enough for young adolescents, many become focused on other aspects of their lives. First of all, bodies elongate, blossom, sprout hair and curves. A girl's self-image over time increasingly depends on the grade she gives her physical appearance, not the grade a teacher marks on a test. School matters less.

This shift has been monitored particularly with regard to girls. In a 2003 survey called *The Strength Girls Have Been Looking For: The Secret to Self-Esteem,* 66 percent of girls between the ages of twelve and fourteen said that their opinion of themselves is tied to how well they do in school. Little more than a third admitted self-esteem is tied to what they weigh and how they look. By the time girls hit between fifteen and seventeen, school grades mattered less, falling in importance to only 58 percent. For nearly half of those older adolescents, how they looked determined the opinion they held of themselves.

If you think of the change in the light of how those phases of development affect girls, these results make sense. Younger girls want to fit in and so how they do in school academically actually places them in a group. Older girls focus less on peers and more on that capacity for loving. They want to have a relationship with a boy. So they are inclined to try harder to fit the physical standards of beauty—being thin, well-groomed, etc.—that are known to attract boys. And they are more likely to feel unsure that their appearance will measure up. But keep in mind that age alone doesn't determine how much time girls spend thinking about boys or their looks. Development and boy craziness hit unevenly.

These statistics don't mean that all high achievers are destined to trade in textbooks for *The South Beach Diet.* Or that good middle school grades will ultimately go downhill. This study merely underlines how other issues impinge on single-minded thinking about academics.

Parents might also consider research on how wanting to be popular can compete with academic honors. Temple University professor of psychology Laurence Steinberg, PhD, conducted a major study of 20,000 middle and high school students and their families for his book *Beyond the Classroom*. In exploring why school performance slips during these years, Steinberg focused on the home lives, personal choices, and habits of his subjects. When he polled kids about which cliques they aspired to join, only one in ten wanted to run with the brainy crowd, compared to nearly one third who opted for the partying popular kids. He tallied that only 15 percent of his subjects read for pleasure five hours a week while a solid third spent at least five hours partying.

If your preteen appears less motivated to complete her schoolwork, see if she is falling under the influence of a group that downplays academics. Keep the social equation in mind: If good grades are important to her circle of friends, she will keep up good grades and maybe even work harder. Conversely, if good grades are deemed dorky or nerdy, she may deliberately slack off. When an older adolescent's grades dip, chances are she's knee-deep in relationship trouble.

You do need to continue monitoring your daughter's school progress and to maintain high expectations, but temper your pressure with understanding. Help her focus on her larger, long-range goals such as becoming a teacher or a marine scientist. In this way, school will seem more relevant.

## Crazy Little Thing Called Love

Obsessing over finding that one true love and figuring out how to survive all by herself—these and other romantic riddles stress girls. Why not ease those fears? You can by letting her in on many new scientific theories. When you give her correct information early on, you bring her closer to getting her heart's desires and, even more important, you show her how to cope when her plans don't materialize.

Think of what follows as a curriculum about how romance works and how relationships typically unfold. The "lessons" are geared to alleviate some of your girl's insecurity. To make this information understandable to preteens, we have tried to gear the knowledge toward girls' lives.

## Where Is the Love?

Will your daughter find that special someone, she wonders. How? Where? If your little girl follows in the footsteps of today's twenty-somethings, she will remain clueless about the whereabouts of Mr. Right and blame herself when he doesn't pop up in her path bearing a diamond ring and a marriage proposal. Social historian Barbara Dafoe Whitehead, PhD, codirector of the National Marriage Project at Rutgers University, studied the current generation of well-educated, hardworking young adult females who complain that they can't find a man to marry. Apparently Bridget Jones and her diary and many other chick-lit books echo and bemoan a phenomenon to which many relate: the scarcity of eligible men.

Whitehead's book *Why There Are No Good Men Left* delves into the man shortage. The trouble (and the remedy) comes down to proximity. In past decades, girls used college as the place to find a mate. Logistically, that made perfect sense. College campuses teemed with young, single men. In our current world, young college-age women tend to postpone husband hunts. They see college as the means to their professional goals. Of course, many coeds have active love lives, but they don't expect the boyfriends they hook up with or fall for to be forever. It has become acceptable and common for girls to do graduate work, get established in the work world, and marry later.

How young women prioritize their lives now makes sense career-wise. Unfortunately, the wait-to-marry approach also handicaps many of them. Unlike the university setting that crawls with eligible men, the work world contains men of all ages. That translates to far fewer peers. Singles mix in with married men, divorcés, widowers, and confirmed bachelors. For a young woman ready to settle down, finding the right candidate becomes harder. This doesn't so much mean that all the good men are gone, but rather that the search has become more complicated compared to her mother's generation.

Both twenty-somethings and tweens can feel better when they comprehend that there is a geography, a logistics, to romantic happiness. Mr. Right has not become an endangered species.

An old study suggested that the majority of people end up marrying someone who lived within three blocks of them. Since then, people have become more mobile. Yet proximity apparently still guides love matches. For instance, psychology theorists have concluded that the people you see every day start looking better to you. Those familiar neighbors, work associates, commuters, the regular cast of players in daily life, become more and more appealing in the romantic sense. In other words, familiarity may breed contempt, but it also breeds sexual attraction. Love is right in your own backyard, so to speak.

Ask your daughter to test out this backyard theory. Have her look at her current crush or the boys her girlfriends hang with or ogle. Does she hear, "I didn't like him at first but then I found out he liked me and he grew on me"? Does the boy she can't stop thinking about happen to sit next to her in homeroom? Do they take the same school bus? Was he just a friend until she found herself his biology lab partner? Did they meet, perhaps, in the youth group at church or during the community food drive?

Middle school life is full of boys, and since nearness favors her odds, love will ignite for her. A girl who realizes that she is in the right place and that romance is close at hand feels more hopeful instantly.

## Somewhere Out There . . . How Will I Find My Soul Mate?

In 2001, the Gallup Organization surveyed twenty- to twenty-nine-year-olds about their romantic beliefs. A huge majority (88 percent) believed there is one special person out there . . .

waiting. And 94 percent of the females felt intent on finding their "soul mate." This elusive yet unique Mr. Right persona served as the first and foremost quality they sought in a marriage partner. The young women dismissed other qualities such as a male's suitability as a parent, his ability to earn a living, and the commonality of religious views.

Historically speaking, never before have so many young women expected so much from a one-and-only male and from romance! Fifty or sixty years ago, most high school and college-age people responded to survey questions about marriage by saying that they wanted to get married to have a family or to own a home. That generation did not intend to wed exclusively for passion or to land some magical other half in order to feel complete. That famous "You complete me" line sputtered by Tom Cruise in the film *Jerry Maguire* would not have meant anything to them.

The soul mate version of love is new, says Paul Amato, Penn State University professor of sociology, demography, and family studies. Marriage is envisioned currently as the vehicle for self-fulfillment and happiness. If you think that's because women no longer need a man to provide for them, that's not entirely true. It often takes two providers today to keep a family satisfied.

In our sessions with tweens and teens, we heard the soul mate fantasy again and again. One sophomore said, "Girls fall in love with this idea of being in love. People become obsessed with finding and having a soul mate because they hear it and see it over and over again." Remember that from our chapter on movies?

In the real world, some people find one true love, but many more have a number of special romances. Look at the marriage, divorce, remarriage, and serial marriage rate. Finding a true love is not like finding some needle in a haystack.

In our discussions we asked the girls whether or not believing in soul mates was a good idea. Listen to their thoughtful comments and share them with your daughter. A fourteen-year-old said, "In middle school, a girl thinks 'this is it,' 'he's the one.' That is definitely *not* what's going to happen to her. Guys are going to come and go in her life." Another added, "Girls need to be prepared. If you think he's your soul mate, think about what could happen in the future, what about the worst-case 'ifs'? He could cheat on you. He could break up with you. They shouldn't think that 'now that I'm in love, my life is perfect forevermore.' "

Others warned girls about the dangers lurking when you bestow soul mate status on a boy. When a girl jumps to absolute certainty that he is the one, she may jump into sexual activity too fast. When things don't work out, a girl who thinks she has found her once-in-a-lifetime guy, and lost him, may think her life is over.

Help her scale back ultrafantastic notions. How? Bring up the following survey that highlights ordinary romantic gestures. Little things mean a lot and deliver a great deal of romantic pleasure. According to a Harris Interactive poll from 2003, teens answered the "What's romantic?" question this way:

Asking someone to be your Valentine (53 percent)
Having a radio station dedicate a song (51 percent)
Going to a romantic movie (50 percent)
Going to a dance together (48 percent)
Getting or giving jewelry (48 percent)
Exchanging rings (47 percent)

While you are carpooling, or as you pass snacks at a sleepover, ask what girls find romantically rewarding. Use the information to make conversation while standing on line at the movie theater. Emphasize how ordinary loving gestures are wonderful. A reality-based simple context goes a long way in diluting soul mate–type thinking. Promising your daughter that she will probably find more than one love takes a great deal of pressure off. Meeting a boy who will be her Valentine or dance partner will be easier to manage than holding out for that magical soul mate man. And in the here and now, she can look forward to having a favorite song or getting the gift of a heart-shaped locket. The best plus, though, comes from knowing that she may have more than one beau to look forward to hugging and kissing and loving.

## How Can I Be Sure?

Falling in love can be gradual or immediate. Love can feel euphoric, or like contentment, or be pure longing. Young adolescents have difficulty understanding emotions to begin with and so getting an accurate read on love can be daunting.

Suggest your daughter always ask herself why she is attracted to someone. His hair or his sense of humor could be reasons. A more complicated explanation of infatuation is stress.

Without getting too technical, stress triggers the same chemicals that love ignites. The body has the same physiological responses to both: a quickened pulse and a racing heart, for example. And so infatuation can feel the same as terror. It's not surprising that the two often become confused. This phenomenon has been called the Stockholm syndrome. In 1973, four Swedes imprisoned in a bank vault by bank robbers became attached to their captors. A similar event you may remember is the Patty Hearst story. Kidnapped by the Symbionese Liberation Army, Patty evolved. She began her captivity as a terrorized heiress used as bait by her captors. Then she developed feelings for one of them and wound up on the nightly news brandishing a gun and joining in during a bank heist.

Danger and attachment go hand in hand. A college junior told us, "My relationship with Matt began during the hurricane emergency that hit our campus. As a category four storm headed our way, we were all confined to our dormitories. The cafeteria closed and issued us brown-bag rations. We received instructions to bring our bedding out into the hallways to clear the windows in our rooms in case high winds broke the glass. That's the weekend I began seeing my boyfriend."

Have your daughter do a little detective work in order to see if this principle holds true. Does she know teammates who became a couple during a competition? Has a tragedy happened in the community and has it brought people together? Emergencies happen. When we feel scared it's natural to seek comfort and safety in someone's arms. There are times when stress can lead to a relationship that will work out fine, but it's not always the case. After 9/11, stories surfaced revealing how some widows of firefighters who died fell in love with surviving firefighters who spent extra time consoling them. Divorces and remarriages sometimes followed.

When a person knows beforehand how stress can be at the root of an infatuation, she is forewarned. A woman contemplating an affair when she is under stress can weigh her reactions and actions. A worker in a company that's gripped in scandal or downsizing can be prepared for feeling emotionally attached to a fellow coworker. And in the world of preteens, two students on the chess team who become a couple during the championships can understand why they want to play chess together day and night.

## Will You Still Love Me Tomorrow?

Nineties boy bands such as the Backstreet Boys croon about promises of everlasting love and, in the next breath, wonder if anybody stays in love anymore. Love can seem, like a bubble, easily breakable. Or like a tornado, barely predictable. How can you explain to a romantic novice how concrete love can be? Show her the concrete side. Explain that love is an emotion, but it is also an action verb.

Maintaining a healthy romantic relationship popularly gets chalked up to compatibility. If two lovers have similar personalities and values, if they both enjoy sports and hate clutter, it is generally assumed their odds for long-term love are better. The fly in that ointment, though, is that opposites with little in common also attract.

Which is it? Successful marriages have come under scrutiny

recently and the results have yielded a few surprises. More than one expert has concluded that compatibility promises little for long-term success. Diane Sollee, founder and director of Coalition for Marriage, Family, and Couples Education says in *Psychology Today,* "There's no such thing as a compatible couple. All couples disagree about the same things: money, sex, kids, time. So it's really about how you manage your differences. If there is chemistry, then the whole courtship is about convincing yourself and others that you are compatible. But, really, you create compatibility."

Sollee has company. "My research," insists Ted Huston (quoted in the same magazine), a psychology professor who runs the PAIR project, a longitudinal study of marriages, "shows that there is no difference in the objective level of compatibility between couples who are unhappy and those who are happy."

What accounts for lasting satisfaction then? What ensures love everlasting turns out to be more about how couples behave. Successful happy pairs commit to each other. They act caring. They practice compassion, patience, and forgiveness. Love affairs that last ground themselves in reality, not fantasy.

Teaching young adolescents about proximity, about stress, and about working at relationships cannot guarantee that nothing will go wrong. Tween romances will end. Even the most promising ones can fail.

## Heartbreak Hotel:
## What Becomes of the Brokenhearted?

Let's not forget that tween romances typically tend to be short-lived. They can last two weeks or two days. The teen landscape is littered with girls whose hearts have been broken. And there are still more who haven't had the chance to love and lose that boy of their daydreams.

Do broken hearts hurt young adolescent lovers more deeply? Actually, they do. Love can be more devastating for the young. Compared to adults, young adolescents are novices at handling the lows of romantic mishap—jealousy, hurt, betrayal, self-consciousness, frustration, and despondency.

For starters, hormones tend to exaggerate the low feelings that accompany romantic rejection. And while adolescent brains can cognitively think through breakups, they do not always do so rationally. Most boys and girls can't put broken romances into proper perspective. For one thing, tweens are known for judging themselves rather harshly. This actually has to do with the emergence of their conscience. Around thirteen, conscience becomes more fully formed. Young adolescents spend a great deal of time weighing ethics, and judging becomes a large part of that process. Like toddlers learning to walk and being preoccupied with a staircase, preadolescents are vulnerable to overjudging.

They obsess. Add the fact that immature brains are inexperienced at managing the emotions, reactions, and responses swirling around getting dumped. When a boy breaks your daughter's heart, it feels like the end of the world. Preteens, especially, live in the present, and feel imprisoned in a melancholy dungeon from which there appears to be no way out.

Being rejected at twelve, thirteen, or fourteen is bad enough, but it is worse in your child's eyes because everyone at school knows or will know. Middle schoolers are notoriously self-conscious. They feel that everyone is watching them all the time, even when that may not be the case. And don't forget how a girl's reputation and social standing can dive after the gossip mill gets going. No wonder the aftermath of romance proves so embarrassing and hits so hard.

The fact that children engage in sexual acts at younger ages—oral sex, hooking up, sexual intercourse—only adds more emotional fuel to the coupling fires, and more crash and burn when it's over. (We will talk more about sex in chapter 7.)

When your child hurts, there are strategies you can rely on to help a brokenhearted girl mend. Don't think this means you can start right away. Her emotions may be so raw she may need time to cry and to grieve on her own before she lets you in. A good rule of thumb is to stay close, stay quiet, and give her plenty of hugs.

**Use the healing power of your nurturing.** A survey done by Kara Joyner out of Cornell University and J. Richard Udry of the University of North Carolina at Chapel Hill of 8,200 kids (ages twelve to seventeen) found that the romantically involved showed a bigger increase in depression levels than the romantically uninvolved. Girls suffered more than boys. Broken hearts were a main source.

What made depression worse? A teen who felt a deteriorating relationship with parents. In other words, your love really can make up for losing the love of a boy, at least to some extent. So after a breakup, don't get into fights. Avoid the "I told you so" trap. If she doesn't want to open up to you, be patient. Offer, "I know things didn't work out, and I just want you to know I'm here if you want to talk, or when you want to share, or maybe just to devour a dish of chocolate ice cream together."

When she's hurting, find ways to spend time together. In this way you fill the hours that she used to spend with her boyfriend. Never underestimate the value of cliché-sounding standard advice. A sad girl may not bounce back instantly to "If he didn't see in you what I do, then he isn't good enough for you. He's not worth crying over." Nevertheless, such statements will help.

**Acknowledge the strong emotions she feels.** Guide her to the issues beneath her hurt. Work through any nagging questions she may have. *What did I do wrong?* Maybe she did nothing wrong. Young love comes and goes. Repeat that to her. If she has made a mistake, let her talk her way through to that conclusion. Perhaps she acted too cloying or jealous. Let her "own" her mistakes. Don't make excuses about them or dismiss them. That may make her feel better in the short term, but it prevents her from learning. Explain that everyone makes these kind of missteps.

Build with this important corollary: romantic disaster creates opportunity. This is your cue to reveal your broken-heart memory. A mother from Florida offered her example of how her heartbreak turned positive. She said, "My being dumped unfolded a lesson. Letting him go wasn't easy. It wasn't what I wanted. Still, a wonderful experience arose from this painful one. Shortly afterward, I met my husband."

**Address how you can't control someone else's feelings.** *What can I do to get him back?* Girls will try anything to keep a guy or get him back. They can be oblivious to the reality that this never works. Talk about girls you know who tried unsuccessfully to turn back the clock on a failed relationship. Did they beg, plead, or stalk? It's a tough lesson to learn, but necessary.

If you think your daughter is scheming to change his mind, try to help her see the futility of these schemes.

**Unlock the secret about the inability to let go.** *How can I live without him?* Suppose your daughter can't move on from a hopeless crush on a boy who notices her sometimes and ignores her most of the time. Or worse, suppose she had a great boyfriend and now the relationship is over. "Love Stinks" has become her theme song. She mopes or sulks in a mournful haze and can't stop thinking about him or IMing her friends about him.

Unrequited love can be powerful. What makes a person hold on to a heartbreak or a heartbreaker? A term exists for this type of romantic stranglehold, *limerence*. Limerence feels like an addiction. According to psychologists, when the conditions of uncertainty and hope coexist, a person becomes unable to walk away. That slight, topsy-turvy chance of happiness keeps a person hanging on. To get free, a girl has to face up to the fact that there is no hope. She needs courage to leave behind illusions and those "if onlys." Then she can begin to heal.

**Point a brokenhearted girl to tomorrow.** There's more than one fish in the sea. Another love is right around the corner.

Broken hearts come and go. These kinds of messages free a girl from heartbreak hotel.

## Am I the Kind of Girl Boys Fall in Love With?

Nearly all girls look at themselves and wonder if they have what it takes to attract a boy. During early adolescence almost every girl sees only her flaws in her mirror. She's too tall, towering over all the boys. Or she's not developed enough yet. Girls still devour the book *Are You There God? It's Me, Margaret* thirty-five years after it was published because Margaret's issues with bras and entering puberty are timeless. Classmates who develop early have it no better. They brood because their breasts are too large and the only thing boys see when they look.

The insecurities don't confine themselves to physical attributes. Smart girls sometimes think their brains may hurt their appeal. The assumption that boys don't like to be outdone or outsmarted is as old as hula hoops and poodle skirts. We noted earlier that the majority of teens do not rush to join the brainy bunch. Do girls still try to "dumb down" so as not to show up a hot guy? In some circles, more than many would like to admit, young adolescent girls are still vulnerable to belittling their brains. On the one hand, academic achievement has become extremely important for females. Schools, society, parents, and girls themselves have high scholastic goals. And yet . . . If you suspect that your daughter feels torn about what a boy wants in the brains department, remind her to be herself. A boy who is easily intimidated by a smart girl like her is not the boy she will feel comfortable with.

Whenever we sat with parents and the subject of intelligent girls came up, parents always insisted being smart served as an asset. "I advise my daughter, 'You are smart. Don't let anybody tell you any differently!' " exclaimed one mother. Another defender added, "Always use your head and make good choices with it."

Are mothers and fathers on the mark? We compared what adults had to say with what college-age women thought. A college coed said, "My words of advice to younger girls: Never dumb down in order to fit in. Do what you know is right despite what might be 'cool' to your peers because following the crowd is one of *the least intelligent things there is.*"

But some admitted that there's a bit of truth to the idea that "nerdy" girls have fewer boyfriends. A Texas-born coed steamed, "I have a lot to say about this topic because it's been pretty significant in my life. I'm nearly twenty-one and just got my first boyfriend a month ago. I never dated in high school, was never even asked out by a guy, and I've always been smart—the top of the class in most situations. Coincidence? I think not. I've had guy friends who I've been close with, but always felt more like 'one of the guys' than a girl. My intelligence and academic success led guys to ask for my help on things, but they only used me for my skills and never bothered to get to know who I really am."

This may be the twenty-first century, but if Neanderthal thinking threatens to make your accomplished girl doubt herself, reassure her with this young women's suggestion:

> If a girl feels out of the social loop, I'd say bide your time. If she is lucky enough to find that group of smart wacky friends, she'll have no problems. If, like me, she grows up in a homogeneous and closed-minded atmosphere, she'll have to be on her own for a while. It might take you a while, but if you are true to yourself and foster your own abilities then you will find a person who appreciates them and wouldn't want you to change.

A final thought came from a male college student: "Should she dumb down? It all depends on what she's looking for. People are attracted to whomever they feel comfortable around. I can think a girl is drop-dead gorgeous, but if her idea of good conversation is 'how much I love shoes' and mine is 'how artist

A compares to artist B' neither of us will be very comfortable and the attraction will fade."

A smart girl will find someone who values her for her intelligence.

Actually, statistics now exist to prove as much. Men do not shy away from marrying educated high achievers. Sociologist Scott South of the State University of New York at Albany examined what men, both white and of color, found most desirable in a mate. These nineteen- to thirty-five-year-old men were *more* willing to marry a woman with more education than they had, not less willing. They valued a woman's ability to hold a steady job *more* than her age, previous marriages, maternal status, religion, or race.

Remind your daughter that if she is smart it will pay off for her.

Whether a girl possesses brains, outer or inner beauty, charm or talent, she may not truly give herself credit. That's where you come in. Continue to point out how she is the kind of person a boy would be lucky to have as a girlfriend.

## Getting Across: You Are a Natural

Tweenagers get embarrassed as their bodies begin to give off more pungent smells. Here's a lesson on the lighter side. Share with your child that she possesses a hidden romantic asset and skill: her nose.

Human beings are designed to sniff out mates. Every person has a unique immune system found in the DNA that carries its own distinct odor. Human scents are a basis of attraction. Men and women are programmed aromatically to certain others, another way nature strengthens the species to resist disease. And females are more aromatically driven, subtly but powerfully. (Haven't you ever wrapped yourself in that special someone's shirt, breathing in his smell?)

Brown University assistant professor of psychology Rachel

Herz found that the way a man smells to a woman is her second most important criterion (the first is a pleasant disposition), trumping a man's appearance, voice, and muscle tone.

Tell your daughter as long as she has a heart and a nose, she is already a natural.

# CHAPTER 7

# Doin' It and Doin' It and Doin' It and Doin' It

*Teaching Our Daughters About Sex*

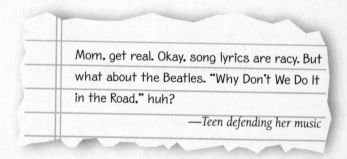

> Mom, get real. Okay, song lyrics are racy. But what about the Beatles. "Why Don't We Do It in the Road," huh?
>
> —*Teen defending her music*

We wanted *Boy Crazy!* to be about romance and relationships, not solely about sex. Nearly everything written or spoken pertaining to adolescent love comes down to talking about sex. Oral sex. AIDS. Hooking up. Teen pregnancy. Rarely do discussions attempt to put sex into any context. The problem lies herein: when we, well-intentioned parents and expert after expert, focus only on sex, we fail to teach our young about the magic of love, its tenderness, its complexities, its passions, and its emotions. Our tweens are left with little but technical sexual information in a sexualized culture that glamorizes "doin' it."

No book on romance though would be complete without frank talk about the sexual landscape a young adolescent faces and how to honestly and effectively talk to daughters about sex. So here we are, poised for sex talk.

In a perfect world, none of us would have to face our tweens and stammer through the dreaded sex talk. We would have had little conversations here and there with our children, starting when they toddled around. Perfect parents read sex education primers early and heeded the advice of the counselors. During a walk on the beach, their four-year-old would say, "Look at the horseshoe crabs playing piggyback." Mom and Dad would exchange a look and one would say nonchalantly, "They are not playing a game; they are mating to have babies." Year by year, bit by bit, these parents added more, replaced words like "my wee-wee" with the correct anatomical word, *penis*. By the time early adolescence came around, their lucky offspring had been seamlessly educated about sexuality.

If you managed that, take a bow. The rest of us failed to be so thorough.

As parents of young adolescents, we, too, needed information and advice in this area, and so we set out to equip ourselves for the sake of our children. Over the last decade, we have monitored the scope of typical tween and teen forays into sexual behavior. We interviewed sex education trainers and counselors. We picked up invaluable insights and ways to make talking about sex easier. So, if you need to play catch-up now, read on.

There are basic ways to handle passing on to your tween specific data and statistics about what goes on among young people. There are opportunities for targeting the right topics to your child as she grows into older adolescence. We'll help you stop stammering and start guiding.

## Not a Girl, Not Yet a Woman

The logical starting point is puberty. Puberty feels frightening because it threatens girls with so many unknowns. Ten- to fifteen-year-olds obsess about their bodies because they stand smack in the middle of enormous physical changes. Girls wonder: When will I get my period? Will I get cramps? How big will my breasts get? Will I tower over all the boys in my class? Girls find themselves curious, anxious, eager, and resistant, sometimes all at once.

As a parent, you can defuse some of your daughter's panic with simple explanations. You can sit her down and explain the details of puberty and menstruation. Or you can go to any bookstore or library and find a book that can provide her with answers to any questions she may have. Basically, she needs to understand that puberty triggers chemical substances that cause her body to change from a girl's into a woman's.

Every girl's body listens to its own clock, but a typical range exists for most of the physical changes. Breasts begin to bud anywhere from the age of eight to thirteen. Pubic hair sprouts. A growth spurt of added height and curves happens afterward. The first menstruation typically occurs around age twelve. But statistics say that girls can start their periods anywhere from ten to fifteen. And some girls of color might begin experiencing some of these changes as early as seven.

A way to approach menstruation casually is to focus on your child's comfort. Tell her that you want to explain hygiene and the use of sanitary napkins so that she can feel prepared in case she gets her first period at school. Explain that budding breasts can chafe against clothing and offer to shop with her for comfortable undergarments. There are so many bra and camisole styles from which to choose.

Don't expect your daughter to be delighted with her bodily metamorphosis. Some girls are; many are not. Warn her that she may experience a host of powerful feelings, especially irritability, before her monthly cycle of menstruation begins.

When we were young girls, few of us got anatomy lessons. Today, in health class girls learn about ovulation, female reproduction, and anatomy—the vulva, clitoris, vagina, and ovaries. The main point you want to get across is that a girl's body is a truly amazing creation. Females struggle with accepting how they look, but every single body regardless of shape or size is a miracle. Preview the fact that as time goes by, that body of hers will serve as her love machine, her sex machine, and, most likely, her baby-making machine.

If she's curious about male puberty, offer her some information. Between the ages of nine and thirteen, testes begin to enlarge. On average, at age twelve, a boy's penis starts to grow. As sperm production increases, boys ejaculate. The first incidence is usually around age thirteen, and it often happens during the night, which is called a "wet dream." From ten to sixteen, boys' height spurts. Facial hair emerges and voices deepen (and crack) typically between twelve and fifteen.

Along with puberty's hormones come sexual urges and feelings toward others. So discussions about menstruation and puberty can naturally flow into guidance and Q&As surrounding sexual topics, for example, that the penis penetrates the vagina, that the sperm unites with the egg. Once a girl knows the mechanics, then you can move on to the more complex layers of sexuality and sexual activity.

## Hooking Up

A fifteen-year-old girl tentatively asked her mom, "What is a prude?"

"Why do you ask?" her mother responded.

The girl huffed, "Jeremy's friends told him I'm a prude because I never hooked up with anyone. I'm not cool."

"Don't you always tell me," this mother recapped, "that those girls who hook up on weekends in the town park after dark are looked down on?"

"Absolutely, they are sluts."

"You know I don't like that term."

"Okay, okay."

Mom continued, "Let me get this straight then. If you do

hook up regularly then you are a bad girl, and looked down upon. If you don't hook up then you are a prude, and looked down upon. Is there a number of hook-ups, say maybe one or two but not more, that give a girl enough experience—but not too much—to be considered a cool girlfriend?"

"Beats me, Mom."

This is a real conversation reported via a New York mother, as exasperated as her maverick child by the impossible maze of tweenage mores. The young adolescent and her adult parent chafed at labels and scratched their proverbial heads regarding the boundary line separating the prude and the slut. Hooking up seems like a damned-if-you-do and damned-if-you-don't social catch-22. If this parent feels confused, if you are confused, imagine how confusing these labels and rules are for ten- and eleven-year-olds.

When your daughter says "hooking up," what does it mean? A refresher from our dating chapter says it depends. It can mean two thirteen-year-olds making out at a party or it can mean engaging in oral sex. It can also mean sexual intercourse when used by older teens. It's what used to be called a one-night stand. To determine your daughter's meaning, tune into her phase of development.

The hook-up culture may sound casual, but that does not mean it's simple. Young adolescents are trying to make sense of, and to evaluate, what some of their peers are doing. They are searching for ways to define themselves as sexual creatures. And they are attempting to sort through the labels often applied to girls, *slut* or *prude*, for example. The labels applied to boys, *player* and *wimp*, offer more confusion, mixing the double standard with the idea of masculinity.

The same old moral and hormonal dilemma has dogged girls before. Current stereotypes echo those from earlier decades: the goody-two-shoes, the girl you marry versus the girl you sleep with, the Madonna and the whore. Remember Sandy in the movie *Grease*? Frilly-frocked and innocent didn't get the guy and so Sandy tarts up, donning tight black leather, teasing her hair, and gyrating seductively as her redder lips sing "You're the One That I Want." Danny is wowed with her sexier image.

How sexy is too sexy? How far should girls go? The beat goes on. The debates continue. In the aftermath of the women's movement, females have more freedom, but how much remains an open-ended question. How forward can and can't a girl be? In 2003, *USA Weekend*'s eighteenth Teen Annual Survey polled 37,000 students ranging from sixth- to twelfth-graders online and in partnership with *YM* magazine and YouthNoise.com. According to the results, social etiquette has changed. Ninety percent of girls and 96 percent of boys think it's okay for a girl to call guys. Eighty percent of girls and 90 percent of boys think it's okay for a girl to ask guys out.

Ask your daughter if these numbers sound right to her and her crowd.

This freedom hits an old wall with what happens next. The double standard still wields an impact on girls. And it affects female liberation and libertine behavior. When kids hear a girl has had sex, 38 percent of boys and 54 percent of girls think *less* of her. Compare this with the reputation question with regard to boys. When kids hear a boy has had sex, 27 percent of boys and 56 percent of girls think less of him. Isn't it fascinating to note that girls hold *both* sexes guilty in nearly equal proportion; both sexes are subject to negative judgment.

And yet when the statistics are analyzed further, it becomes clear that the double standard has eroded for some. More than half of boys and nearly all girls admit that they think about the person who's had sex the same way as before they found out.

How many tweens and teens are engaging in sexual acts? New surveys pop up all the time. Here are some numbers:

- Nearly a third of boys (31 percent) and girls (30 percent) between the ages of fifteen and seventeen have had intercourse.
- Fifty-five percent of teens thirteen to nineteen admit to having had oral sex.

- Twenty-one percent of ninth-graders have slept with four or more partners.

Where does your daughter fit into the statistical breakdown? Which side of the double standard is she on? Would she hook up at a party? If she does, will she wake up to a bashed reputation? Will she become a slut overnight or be teased as the latest goody-two-shoes laughingstock prude? Obviously, you need to have more than one conversation with your daughter about all this.

## That's My Prerogative

Discussing sex with children is no easier for most of us post–sexual revolution adults than it was for our parents. Sitting down with a preteen even with the best intentions of having a frank exchange can turn out to be futile. You can become tongue-tied before you get going and chicken out. Or your child might cut you off, equally embarrassed.

Despite reluctance on both sides, adolescents need and want information. A *Time*/MTV poll noted that 41 percent of teens (ages thirteen to eighteen) believe that parents do not adequately teach them about sex. Schools do not offer enough information either, say 43 percent of those teens surveyed.

So commit to preparing your daughter thoroughly on matters of sex. In order to do so effectively, you must prepare yourself first. What are your beliefs about what kinds of sexual intimacies are appropriate for young adolescents? In what context? In other words, what values do you hold?

A "No, not ever" philosphy will only separate the two of you. Here are a few things to keep in mind as you plan your sexual education talks.

- Spend time discussing sexual issues and ethics with your spouse and agree on the values you intend to cultivate within your family. For instance, is premarital sex ever okay? When?

- Always bring emotions into discussions about sex. Say something like this: *You know how happy you feel when a boy asks you out and how hurt you feel when he moves on to another girl? Multiply those feelings a thousand times because that's what sexual activity will do to your emotions. Sex is like the ocean: never underestimate the force of its waves or the pull of its tides.*

- Practice being unflappable. When your eight-year-old asks you about oral sex, don't turn white and snap, "You're too young to know about that!" Even young children have questions and if you don't supply the answers, they will find them elsewhere. "I once asked my mother what cunnilingus was," says a fifteen-year-old girl. "She got so upset, asking me where I'd heard the phrase and why I was asking, that I would never go to her again." Stay calm and answer the question in a way that is appropriate for the child's age. Make it clear that you are glad she came to you and encourage her to continue to do so in the future.

- As your child goes through middle and high school, inquire what she is being taught in school. Some schools are progressive, others more conservative in their sex education programs. If your school district has an abstinence-only program, beware. The rise of oral sex, even anal sex, has been linked by experts to kids wanting to stay "technically" virgins. They decide anything that's not intercourse isn't sex. In some communities, virginity pledges—defined as a vow to postpone sexual intercourse until after marriage—are popular. Jessica Simpson made hers famous. Yet studies show that even committed virgins lapse, and when they don't have the facts about safe sex and contraception they tend to get pregnant. A little virtue can be a dangerous thing for a teenager when the body is likely to overrule the soul on a hot, steamy night.

- Educate your child about contraception options and the

use of condoms to ensure safe sex even as you reiterate your family values about when the appropriate time is for engaging in sexual behavior. No studies ever linked such knowledge with increased sexual activity among teens.

- Lobby your school district to include contraception along with affirmations about abstinence being the only foolproof method to avoid teen pregnancy.

## Girls Just Want to Have Fun . . . Boys Just Want to Have Sex

Starting a conversation about sex is tricky. A useful approach is to let the culture—via magazine articles, newspaper exposés, and television shows—stimulate a back and forth on issues pertaining to sex. You can slip in your values and encourage your child to open up with questions or her observations.

Books and timely magazine pieces regularly delve into current teenage sexual codes of behavior. An assortment of issues lies at your fingertips. Take peer pressure to have sex, for example. Girls worry that if they don't let a boy _____ (fill in the blank according to your child's age: kiss, touch her breasts, go all the way), he'll be lost forever to another, more cooperative girl. Early phase preteens and older adolescents run into this ultimatum-type of reasoning, even though the sex acts on their minds may differ. The right magazine article, clipped and left in your daughter's bedroom, can get the two of you talking about what's right compared to what a girl feels pressured to do. There are many magazines geared to tweens from which to choose, *Seventeen, Teen,* and *Cosmo Girl,* to name a few.

For instance, *Teen People* annually conducts polls guaranteed to capture your child's interest. According to a survey of 1,000 boys between the ages of thirteen and nineteen, 72 percent of teen boys are virgins. Among older boys, ages seventeen to nineteen, 48 percent are. Nearly half, 45 percent, claim to be

## BOY OR GIRL

What are boys like? What are girls like? We offer this exercise from *Boy V. Girl? How Gender Shapes Who We Are, What We Want, and How We Get Along.* At your daughter's next sleepover, pass out copies of this exercise.

### The Boy v. Girl Gender Roll Poll

Can a boy be serious? Can a girl be in charge? Take this quick quiz. Put an *F* (for female) next to the traits you think are more true for girls and women. Put an *M* (for male) next to the traits you think are more true for boys and men. Place an *X* next to the traits you think apply to everyone.

| | | |
|---|---|---|
| independent —— | logical —— | conceited —— |
| helpful —— | leader —— | likable —— |
| cheerful —— | truthful —— | quiet —— |

in no hurry to lose their virginity. Your daughter is bound to have an opinion on those numbers! You can explore whether the boys she knows, even the popular ones, are more innocent than they try to act.

Yes, when it comes to the subject of boys, girls have enormous curiosity. A mom in one of our focus group offered, "My girls 'idealize' boys. They think of all boys as Prince Charming. I have no sons and that means my daughters have no brothers from whom to learn. My girls need to get a look at boys and see them as just human beings. They need to get past the mystique of the opposite sex."

When we listened to what girls had to say, we understood exactly what that mother meant. We heard other stereotypical

| outspoken ___ | messy ___ | serious ___ |
| moody ___ | forgiving ___ | controlling ___ |
| shy ___ | kind ___ | easily hurt ___ |
| athletic ___ | sensitive ___ | gentle ___ |
| loving ___ | risk taker ___ | trusting ___ |
| self-confident ___ | peacemaker ___ | lazy ___ |
| needy ___ | competitive ___ | troublemaker ___ |
| good listener ___ | emotional ___ | assertive ___ |

Do you have more Fs than Ms, or more Xs? The truth is that everybody, boy or girl, could use a little more or less of these character traits to help them get along and appreciate what makes each of us unique and interesting.

labels, such as *players* and *heartbreakers.* "Guys have lists!" a girl sneered. All the adolescents in that particular focus group shook their manes vigorously to that insensitive portrayal, affirming a well-understood characterization of the boys they knew. Their consensus was that all boys rate girls as if they were meat, prime cut or substandard. A seventeen-year-old changed the subject but not the tenor with, "Boys definitely have more power to coerce a girl to do things that she may not be ready for." Again heads nodded soberly.

"Boys take getting together with a girl lightly. They're like, 'When you get together, man, do her and stuff.' Guys make bets about who can go the furthest." Sounds like the plotline from a movie. *American Pie,* anyone?

Part of your role as a guide and sex educator is to undo negative stereotypes and to explain to girls more about the opposite sex. Not all boys are cads, callous, or Casanovas. Fathers are obviously well-equipped to do this kind of explaining, drawing boys as well-rounded creatures. Girls need to hear this. If father-daughter conversations are not likely, then mothers should fill in.

Where do you get good information about what boys are really like? Go to a good book about boys, and introduce what you learn as dinner conversation. To get you started, here are a few snippets from three books, guaranteed to spark chatter.

**Why are boys loath to act lovingly?** The nonchalant or thoughtless way boys act toward them when in the company of other boys befuddles girls. In *Raising Cain: Protecting the Emotional Life of Boys,* Dan Kindlon, PhD, and Michael Thompson, PhD, say, "At about the same time that boys are beginning to develop sexually and develop an interest in girls, they are subjected to a culture of cruelty, which is all about power, dominance, and denial of sensitivity. A boy is taught in a systematic way to view his tender feelings as 'feminine' and to eschew them." Doesn't this describe exactly how Danny in the beginning of *Grease* behaves toward Sandy in front of his friends? One minute, he acts giddy and guileless, so glad to see her, his summer romance. He didn't expect her to enroll in his high school. Then he glances at his buddies, does an about-face and turns macho and rude.

**Are boys born to cheat?** We've all read about the umpteen species of monkeys, apes, or orangutans who inseminate as many females as they can to ensure the survival of the species. The assumption carried down the Darwinian ladder is that all males are promiscuous. Surprise, surprise! It seems that male anthropologists may have been biased.

In *Same Difference: How Gender Myths Are Hurting Our Relationships, Our Children, and Our Jobs,* Rosalind Barnett, a senior scientist at Brandeis University, and Carly Rivers, a professor and journalist, review much research and discover that seed-sowing to lots of suitors is common within female species, too. It seems that since female anthropologists have entered the field, they have been refuting sexist assumptions, namely that old notion that would-be mommies only mate with one male.

**How do boys in love act?** William Pollack, PhD, in his book *Real Boys,* offers theories that you can put out there for dinner-time enlightenment and debate. For starters, he argues, " 'Boys will be boys' is not said when a little boy brings a present to his teacher or gives his crying mother a hug. Or when a teenage boy obviously feels racked with guilt for breaking up with his girlfriend. Or when an older boy spends time with a dying parent in the hospital." Boys show their love with actions, he says, "Rather than telling his mom how much he loves her on Mother's Day, the boy may instead simply ask her if she'd like to go to the movies with him that day."

Boys work at affection. Boys are protective when they care about someone. See if your kids have noticed any of this. Do boys perform labors of love such as taking out the garbage, painting the kitchen, building a trellis in the garden? Isn't a boy caring when he shovels snow off the sidewalk so his mother or grandmother won't fall on the ice?

Girls benefit greatly when you expand their knowledge of what boys are truly like and how they act in relationships. They need to hear and understand that boys are not all after one thing. There's more to young males than the stereotypes.

## Papa, Don't Preach. Watch TV Instead

Television gets sexier all the time. R-rated movies replay end-lessly. There are erotic plotlines on daytime soaps and night-time dramas and across many channels. The Henry Kaiser Family Foundation found that the percentage of shows depict-

ing or implying sexual intercourse rose from 10 percent in the
1999–2000 season to 14 percent in the 2001–02 season. The
rate spiked higher among the twenty shows most popular with
teenage viewers. Isn't *Friends* (endlessly syndicated) almost always about who's sleeping with whom?

The boom in reality shows, such as *Temptation Island* and
*The Bachelorette,* added more steam. The Parents Television
Council analyzed this genre (namely the first four episodes
from June 2002 to August 2003) and concluded that viewers
saw per hour on average 492 instances of sex—either visual or
implied.

What's a parent to do? Turn off the TV? No. Capitalize on all
these sexy scenarios. Target specific shows to watch with your
daughter and critique the romantic actions. Do the vixens and
hunks on *One Tree Hill* suffer consequences after sex? Should
couples on *The O.C.* sleep together? Even Joan from *Joan of Arcadia,* who regularly gets instructions from God, can't rely on
her direct spiritual line to escape the teen angst that goes along
with her free will to decide whether or not she should go all the
way.

*Everwood,* in particular, where the fathers of the teen characters are doctors, presents frequent story lines that revolve
around sexual decision making and its risks. Character development shows how sexual intercourse can lead to repercus-
sions, such as an unwanted pregnancy. Contraception and safe
sex get airtime. As you mull over Ephram's affair with an older
college-age singer, or Amy's decision to get the pill, you can slip
in a fact or two about sexually transmitted diseases (STDs)
such as AIDS and the HIV virus, and sexually transmitted in-
fections (STIs), including chlamydia, herpes, and genital warts,
to name a few. Here are some facts:

- STIs and STDs are spread by sexual contact through se-
  men and vaginal secretions—that means oral sex, too.
  This point needs to be made with your daughter. As a
  teen girl explained, "Oral sex . . . it's not sex. We don't

call it that. It's as if, if we take out the sex word, it's not sex. We call it something else—giving head, blow job."

- Every year 3 million sexually active teens acquire an STI—in other words one in four. For more information consult a good resource such as *How to Talk with Your Teens About Love, Relationships, and S-E-X* by sex educators Amy G. Miron, M.S., and Charles D. Miron, PhD.

Watch for cable TV movies that touch on AIDS. Today's young people have no memory of the plague two decades ago (yes, it has been that long) that decimated the gay community. In that time, new strains of the HIV virus, the precursor to AIDS, have emerged. Actually, more people are infected than ever before, though there is a lower death rate because of more effective drugs.

Tuning in together to the love lives of your favorite television romantics can be fun. Every new television season offers family dramas that can provide fodder for your mutual entertainment and opportunities for parents to slip in sexual guidance.

## All the News That Gives Us Fits . . . Gives Us Opportunity

Keep an eye out for articles that skirt, or even sensationalize, issues that are relevant to sex and teens. For example, a May 23, 2004, article in the *New York Post*, "Kids' Cuff Kink," described a "bizarre new kids' sex craze sweeping the city's elementary schools." According to the story, girls as young as eleven stack colorful bracelets on their arms, each hue representing a different sex act from a deep kiss to oral sex. When a boy snaps a bracelet off a girl, the article continues, it is considered to be essentially a coupon good for that sex act.

The story implies that this is a trend sweeping the city. Factually speaking, only two schools, a Catholic school in Queens and a public school in the Bronx, actually emerged in the copy as sources. Pressing the girls at those schools for details decreased the implications further. The eleven-year-old who sold the bracelets to her classmates at the Catholic school backpedaled by later claiming that "neither she nor any of her friends are actually having sex."

Such journalism may be questionable in the accuracy department. Nevertheless, passing along a basic story line like this (even a hysterical one) to your preteen serves as a lively conversation starter. You could ask whether or not these bracelets are in fashion. Are sexually explicit sex acts tied to a girl's popularity? From there, your daughter may tell you what girls are doing. Now you have a space in which to flesh out her questions and to inject your own values about casual sex.

The issue at the center of this next exposé skews better for teenage girls in later phases of love. A January 19, 2003, article in the *Washington Post,* "The Buddy System," profiled coeds who lacked steady beaus but obviously not healthy libidos. Young women at several of the finest universities, such as Brown, Cornell, and Berkeley, opted to have sexual trysts with boys who were just friends. They wanted no strings, no commitments, no protestations of love, just sexual satisfaction. It made the young women sound like feminist followers of TV's *Ally McBeal,* the yuppie lawyer known for her many sexual escapades. Later in the story, the girls confessed to wanting more—"leisurely strolls, candlelight dinners, small gifts and other gestures of courtship."

This newspaper story again imparts information that you should be aware of. How prevalent is it for friends to indulge in sexual exploration together? Ask your teen: What's love got to do with buddy sex? In both of these cases, the stories (exaggerated or not) highlight the culture's casual attitudes and changing mores with regard to appropriate sexual activity. And examples like these, which aren't hard to find, are very useful and timely.

We've touched on this earlier and it has come up on MTV. In MTV's *The Ashlee Simpson Show,* singer Ashlee chatters back and forth on camera about whether she and Ryan are boyfriend/

girlfriend or "friends with benefits." Such media examples are current and gossipy and don't put your daughter on the spot and so they give her free rein to comment. And they give you the chance to offer guidance. Just be careful not to fall into the next few traps.

**Don't believe everything you read.** Critique the news stories you read. When you see alarming stories involving adolescents, especially if they are local exposés, don't jump to conclusions that the activities are widespread throughout your community. If the story raises questions in your mind, do your own investigating before talking with your daughter. Start with the counselors at her school. Mention the article and even give them a copy. Ask for their reactions. Are they concerned? Have they got any inside information about the activity? Perhaps they have counseled young adolescents having oral sex or they've heard about rampant misconduct. Talk with other parents. Did they see the story? You don't want to stick your head in the sand, but you don't want to assume every headline is ripped from your tweenager's school or circle of friends.

**Avoid knee-jerk reactions.** Headlines can be unnerving. Reading shocking stories may trigger an overreaction on your part. Suppose your preteen came to the breakfast table wearing a colorful stack of bracelets just as you perused that story in the morning paper. Not all tweenagers or teenagers engage in the indiscriminate sexual acts that wind up on the front pages. Calm yourself before impulsively lecturing your daughter. You don't want to sound as if you are accusing her of sexual misconduct. Realize that a convincing journalist stacking salacious anecdotes naturally arouses suspicion that your daughter could be guilty of similar out-of-control behavior, but that you may be jumping to conclusions. Take a few hours, maybe even days, until you are rational enough to proceed.

Find nonconfrontational words such as "I read an interesting story the other day. It said that teens in some schools were . . ." If she doesn't respond immediately, don't assume the worst. Whether she answers or not, find a way to get across your point of view that leaves the door open for future discussion. "I don't know why the kids involved didn't go to their parents," you can say, adding, "I hope if you are in a similar situation, you will come to me."

## Let's Have a Party!

Sex education is not complete until you address the effect of alcohol. Adults, because they themselves drink, are reluctant and confused about what to say. Don't allow guilt to prevent you from broaching the topic. Begin as soon as your child enters middle school because that's when the boy-girl partying begins and takes on electricity. Tweenagers who socialize are prone to feel nervous. Just like many adults, they don't feel comfortable in social situations. Adults use alcohol as the mechanism to lubricate social encounters. When adults want to have sex, many drink because alcohol lowers sexual inhibitions. Teens are following this lead.

Alcohol has become perhaps the most widespread danger affecting adolescents. Its use and abuse puts teen lives and their sex lives at risk. Partying is hot, say the exploits of famous party girls such as Tara Reid and Lindsay Lohan. Your tween may be too young to go clubbing, but parties are part of growing up.

The Internet puts a virtual stamp on getting smashed for fun. Websites exist called Barshots.com, AmIWasted.com, and RateMyVomit.com and show college-age boys passed out, their unconscious bodies dolloped with whipped cream. Such sites incite adolescents to outdo one another with drunken antics. Teens photograph, videotape, and post stupid drunk images. The subliminal message on these sites, according to James Steyer the CEO of Common Sense Media, is "get drunk, get girls, get laid."

The pattern of drinking that goes on today means more than a few beers. According to a report, "Teen Tipplers: America's Underage Drinking Epidemic," put out by the National Center on Addiction and Substance Abuse, more than 5 million high school students binge drink at least once a month. Binge drinking is defined as consuming five or more shots at a time. Tallying ninth-grade boys' alcohol track record and comparing it to girls' indicates that drinking happens among both sexes in nearly equal measure: 40 percent of the boys and 41 percent of the girls imbibed. In the binge drinking category, 22 percent of the boys and 20 percent of the girls downed shot after shot.

Are preteens too young, are their moving-up dances too innocent to be placed alongside tales of drunken exploits? In some instances, yes. However, drinking does occur at younger ages, and younger kids are at greater risk of later alcoholism. Individuals who begin consuming alcohol before the age of fifteen are four times more likely to become dependent, compared to those who take a first taste at twenty-one. Actually the likelihood of lifetime alcohol abuse is greatest for precocious fourteen-year-old alcohol experimenters, says Millie Webb, national president of Mothers Against Drunk Driving (MADD).

Parents have a poor track record when it comes to aggressively punishing youthful alcohol abuse. Some dismiss underage drinking as part of growing up, despite the toll it takes on young people in terms of car crashes, accidents, homicides, suicides, and sexual consequences.

Significant numbers of adults believe in a strategy that could be called "permit and contain." They let their underage children drink under their roof and serve alcohol to minors when the party stays in their homes. Harris Interactive and the *Wall Street Journal* polled 2,019 adults with children between the ages of fifteen and twenty about whether to tolerate teen drinking under parental supervision. A quarter (24 percent) admitted they would allow an older teen to drink if a parent were home. Eleven percent admitted that their teen could attend a party where alcohol would be served so long as a parent was present. Adults estimate that 23 percent of the parents they knew allowed their kids to go to parties where alcohol was served.

What's so bad about this? Underage drinking is against the law for one thing. In some states, social host liability laws make the parent legally culpable for allowing alcohol consumption by minors. And drinking leads to sexual activity.

According to the Centers for Disease Control and Prevention, an estimated 50 percent of fourteen- and fifteen-year-olds get drunk at least once a month. Seventy-nine percent of eighteen-year-olds do the same. These percentages are *the very same* for those in each age group who report being sexually active. Could the link between getting drunk and getting sexually intimate be any clearer?

As a high school senior told us, "Girls drink; I drink. It's easier to put yourself out there socially after a drink. And there's no stigma attached to alcohol, no qualms about admitting that you drink."

Don't cop out about underage drinking or rationalize your way around it.

**Talk to your tweens early and often.** Make the point that underage drinking is illegal. Be firm. Make conversation about the local DWI car accidents that unfortunately happen all the time. Don't you read about a teen in your area who died in an alcohol-related accident at least once a year?

**Supervise all parties.** When your child attends a party, inquire beforehand if an adult will be present because according to statistics one in five tweens between the ages of twelve and fourteen admitted attending a party in the last six months where there were no adults on the premises.

**Practice with your tweens ways to say no.** Peer pressure hits powerfully, so give your child credible language to resist. "My parents would ground me forever if they smelled alcohol on me." "My dad's already told me that if he catches me drinking, he'll never let me get my driver's license."

**Discuss how kids use alcohol as an excuse to hook up.** Point out that using the "I was drunk" excuse may get a girl off the hook temporarily, but such explanations never undo mistakes. You can evade the responsibility for bad decisions, but no one can put a positive spin on a car wreck, unprotected sex, or a ruined reputation.

**Drink responsibly.** As an adult you are entitled to drink. However, you have a responsibility to model appropriate and responsible behavior. Don't drink and drive. Don't drink and operate a boat. If you do drink more than you should and behave badly in front of your tweens or teens, address it the morning after. Adolescents watch adults closely.

## Let's Spend the Night Together

Each generation sings songs about doing "it." We adults, though, didn't grow up with music videos practically showing gyrating teens in the act. Then and now, all young adolescents' minds move toward experimenting with sex. Expect that your daughter will try something between the ages of ten and twenty. Didn't you?

"For high school teens the 'petting party' was the most notorious arena for testing sexual feelings and responses," writes researcher Lucy Rollin in *Twentieth Century Teen Culture by the Decade.* "During the decade, 'necking' came to refer to ardent and prolonged kissing, while 'petting' described many kinds of erotic activity, but usually referred to caresses and fondling below the neck. At petting parties, where couples engaged in these activities with other couples nearby, the group nature of the event provided automatic limits on how far to go."

Rollin is describing petting parties of the 1920s here. The

more things change, the more things stay the same. Throughout every decade young and older adolescents have smooched and groped in parked cars at drive-in movies, in basement playrooms, or on living room couches with music videos blasting. Some inevitably went all the way. Eventually, by the age of twenty-one, a majority did.

In the final analysis, your daughter needs you to advise and inform her about sex. So take a deep breath and start rehearsing.

CHAPTER ♥ 8

# We Are the World, We Are the Children

Dating in a Multiracial Environment

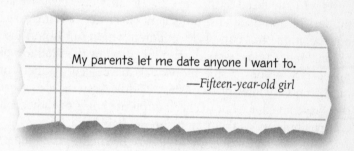

My parents let me date anyone I want to.

—*Fifteen-year-old girl*

What's the chance that your daughter will bring home a boy of a different race or ethnic background? It's more likely than you think. You could wind up living in an updated version of *Guess Who's Coming to Dinner?* In that 1967 classic film, Spencer Tracy and Katharine Hepburn play a couple whose political sensibilities are challenged when their daughter brings home her black fiancé, played by Sidney Poitier. Watch the movie with an adolescent, and he or she is likely to be shocked by the conservative (some might even say racist) approach that prevailed, even in the liberal, free-love sixties.

The updated version of the Poitier classic, *Guess Who?* turned the tables, with Ashton Kutcher playing a white man trying to impress his girlfriend's African-American father, played by Bernie Mac. Young people today are more accepting of dating and marrying across color and ethnic lines. When Gallup asked about interracial dating in 1980, just 17 percent of teens said that they had dated someone of another race, though Hispanics were not included in the count. In 1997, a *USA Today* poll of 602 teens found that 57 percent of those who went out on dates said they had been out with someone of another race or ethnic group, whether white, black, Hispanic, or Asian. By 1999, a survey by American Eagle Outfitters and *Teen People* magazine found that 60 percent were receptive to dating someone of a different ethnic background.

As we look ahead to the next few decades, this inclusive attitude will dominate and ultimately affect not only marriage but the ethnic makeup of the children who result from those unions. Indeed, many children are themselves the products of mixed-race unions. Some individuals have such a variety of racial traits—white, black, Asian, Middle Eastern, etc.—that they have no choice but to check duplicate boxes or "other" on college applications that inquire about their ethnicity.

An increasing number of adults are becoming accepting of biracial dating. A 2004 survey done by *AARP,* a magazine circulated to those over age fifty, found that 71 percent (79 percent of Hispanics, 66 percent of whites, 86 percent of blacks) would not object to a child or a grandchild marrying someone of another race. Yet many parents whose heritage is less complicated cannot help but feel a little bit like Christina and Matt Drayton, the Tracy-Hepburn characters, when their child brings home a love interest whose background is so different from their own.

No race has a monopoly on discomfort. White, black, Hispanic, Indian, Israeli, Middle Eastern, and Asian parents may confront these issues if a daughter chooses from a different cultural world. "My parents would prefer me to be with someone from my own background, because we would have more in common," says one Hispanic girl.

Considering that dating across ethnic lines and cultural barriers has become the reality for many adolescents today, are you comfortable with that? Perhaps you are. Still, our children are way ahead of us.

Even the term *color blind* is obsolete. This fact was pointed out to us when we used the term in a magazine article. Current thinking, rather than trying to ignore differences, suggests that we should acknowledge and appreciate the variety of skin colors. So if you thought you could skip this chapter, think again. We offer these words not to imply that dating across color lines should make you uncomfortable, but rather to upgrade your sensitivity. Not everyone is on the same page.

Even if parents disavow racism, they may worry about how a child will handle cultural differences that impinge on relationships. What guidance can you give your daughter that will help her avoid these pitfalls? How will you soothe her hurt feelings if cultural differences ultimately lead to a breakup? While young adolescents are a long way from serious pairings that might result in marriage, these early encounters can be important and have lasting effects—positive and negative.

As we sought out focus groups of young adolescents and teens with whom to discuss romance, we deliberately included a mixture of cultures and races. From these young people, we heard that many of them encounter roadblocks. Sometimes from family and parents, sometimes from peers. Apparently, we are all at various places on the learning curve with regard to race relations. We need to find out more about one another before we can truly be comfortable.

## Star Power Changes Minds

Superstar Jennifer Lopez has done more to advance the cause of racial diversity than any civics lesson could. Her romantic choices have included an African-American (P. Diddy), a white (Ben Affleck), and finally, the man she married, Marc Anthony, who, like JLo, is Puerto Rican. Divas like Lopez have a huge influence over young people. Adolescent girls eagerly duplicate her hairstyles and dress. Why not her dating patterns?

Lopez is just one star in the mighty constellation that affects our young people. From the movies and TV shows they watch, to the music they listen to, young people are swayed by this culture:

- Advertisements for products popular among young people—Calvin Klein, Benneton, the Gap, Victoria's Secret—play up diversity.
- Black actor Blair Underwood played the love interest of white actor Cynthia Nixon (Miranda) on the popular *Sex and the City.* He had it all: looks, charm, a career as a doctor for the New York Knicks. The story line barely took note of the racial differences between them. Underwood was quoted as observing: "[Race is] a nonissue. I think that's more current in this day and age, when it's not a novelty to see interracial dating on television anymore."
- Jesse L. Martin, a black actor, who moved on to play a cop on *Law & Order,* first burst onto the TV scene playing a love interest of Ally McBeal, the hip lawyer portrayed by white actor Calista Flockhart.
- On the *West Wing,* white President Bartlett's daughter dated her father's black aide.
- Mixed-race actor Halle Berry's characters in the James Bond movie *Die Another Day* and her Academy Award–winning *Monster's Ball* linked up with white men.
- In *Save the Last Dance,* Julia Stiles's character falls in love with an African-American teen, played by Sean Patrick Thomas.
- Disney's animated *Pocahontas* is an interracial dating story for children.
- Formerly lily-white fairy tales now have an ethnic cast. In a 1997 remake of *Cinderella,* the future princess was played by black pop singer Brandy, and her prince played by Paolo Montalban, a Filipino.
- High-profile athletes and stars are multicultural. Golf phenom Tiger Woods claims many races—Caucasian, African-

American, Indian-Asian. Other mixed-race stars include New York Yankees shortstop Derek Jeter, pop singer Mariah Carey, and Miss America 2003, Erika Harold.

## Storming the Color Gates

Releasing the film *Guess Who's Coming to Dinner?* in 1967 turned out to be auspicious. That year, the U.S. Supreme Court, in a unanimous ruling, struck down as unconstitutional laws prohibiting marriages between blacks and whites. In the 1960s, racially mixed marriages represented less than one-half of 1 percent of marriages nationwide. But the picture would begin to change. By 1980, that figure rose to 2.5 percent, and by 2001, according to an article in *Time* magazine, the number of mixed-race marriages more than doubled to 5 percent, or, by some estimates, 6 percent.

Rather than the waffling and concern exhibited by the Tracy-Hepburn characters, biracial couples today meet with less resistance. In a 2001 survey of biracial couples by the *Washington Post,* the Henry J. Kaiser Foundation, and Harvard University, 72 percent of respondents said their families embraced their union immediately. Black and white couples encountered the highest level of disapproval, with two thirds saying that at least one set of parents objected. By latest count, there are only 450,000 black-white marriages in the United States, compared with 700,000 white-Asian, and 2 million white-Hispanic.

Interracial dating and cohabitation is skyrocketing. University of Michigan sociologist David R. Harris says that one in six interracial unions is a cohabitation. The *Washington Post* found that four of every ten Americans said they had dated someone of another race and almost three in ten said it had been a serious relationship.

Besides the youth culture, other factors have made cross-race pairings more possible:

**Heavy immigration of Hispanics and Asians.** This influx has increased chances of meeting people from other racial and ethnic groups.

**Increase in minority enrollment in public schools nationally, to more than 35 percent from 24 percent in 1976.** That change in school population has had an effect. In 2002, Kara Joyner, a sociologist at Cornell University, analyzed data from the National Longitudinal Study of Adolescent Health from 134 schools nationwide, including large city schools to large and small rural schools, with diverse or homogenous populations. She found that nearly one fifth of all surveyed students had had a romantic relationship with someone of a different race during the previous year and a half. Remember love in your own backyard? That obviously extends to the schoolyard too.

**Increase in minority enrollment in colleges.** Again, with more diversity, there is more opportunity to meet and date someone of a different race. In 1999, 7,040 freshman were admitted to the University of Texas at Austin. Of these, 286 were African-American, a 43.7 percent increase from the year before. In addition, 1,212 of the new freshmen were Asian, a 7.4 percent increase; and 974 were Hispanic, up 9.3 percent from 1998. A survey done at East Carolina University found that almost half of the 620 students polled were open to an interracial relationship. Almost a quarter had already dated someone of another race. Those particularly approving were those who were black, had experience in living together, and had dated interracially before.

**Increased acceptance and frequency of interracial marriage.** With legal barriers removed and society's taboos evaporating, mixed-race marriages are increasing. Looking at love through youth-culture eyes, mixed-race marriages are everywhere.

**More diverse workplaces.** Many people hold jobs where those of all races and ethnic backgrounds work and cooperate side by side. In fact, job success is closely linked with being able to work effectively with many different types of coworkers.

**A growing trend in interracial dating services, including telephone and Internet personal ads.** Sites such as Opposites Attract and Ebony and Ivory Together encourage customers to embrace multicultural relationships. *Interrace* magazine, a publication dedicated to multiracial couples and their families, addresses issues such as the best place to live, dating anxieties, and how to combat aggression and stereotypes from others.

Ron Taffel, author of *The Second Family: How Adolescent Power Is Challenging the American Family,* commented on *Time's* 2001 findings on mixed-race relationships: "In adolescent life and culture, kids hang out together in all different kinds of groups. It's what's accepted, what one sees on TV, in the movies, in tons of advertising. Now when kids date interracially, they're not doing it to rebel or upset their parents, but because it's part of life. It's a profound difference." In fact, less than half of teens polled by *USA Today* said they dated interracially to annoy their parents. Ninety-seven percent said they did so because they found the person attractive, 75 percent because they were curious, and 54 percent said they were trying to be different.

## Barriers Still Exist

On November 21, 2004, two interracial couples living in a two-family home in Lake Grove, Long Island, woke up to a frightening sight: a burning cross on their front lawn. Laurie Miller, who is Italian, and her husband, Calvin, who is black, woke up at 3:00 a.m. when someone rang their doorbell. Their upstairs neighbors, Richard Eggert, whose background is a mixture of German, Irish, and Italian, and his fiancée, Rachel Sanchez, who is Puerto Rican, were awakened by the light cast by the flames upon their bedroom walls. When the couples looked out their windows, they were shocked. Their quiet Long Island neighborhood has been racially mixed for a long time. Eggert told the *New York Daily News*: "I was amazed that people are still so ignorant."

This hate crime didn't happen in the Deep South, but in the Northeast, where people are supposedly more liberal and accepting of mixed-race couples. The incident brings home the sad fact that some prejudices die hard. Despite the advances that have been made, race remains a volatile issue in America.

The reaction interracial couples receive depends in large part on where they live. There are more mixed-race couples in cities, university towns, and large states with diverse populations, such as California, Texas, Florida, and New York. Travel off that beaten path and it is possible to run into outright racism.

Not until 2000 were black and white high school seniors at Butler High School in Georgia permitted to dance together in a formal setting. Until that time, two privately organized, segregated proms were held. Some of the older residents still have reservations about mixing the races. Younger people, however, feel differently. "We go to school together, we work together, so why can't we dance together?" one teen asked.

In 2002, Taylor County High School in Albany, Georgia, held its first integrated prom. A year later, white students went back to holding their own prom, while blacks, forced to hold another dance, announced that theirs would be open to everyone. Similarly, in Wrightsville, Georgia, parents at the public high school organized a private, whites-only prom to keep the races separate.

While the whites-only prom situation is an extreme example, students of all ethnic backgrounds still self-segregate. "People feel comfortable with their own kind," one girl explains. As adolescents see it, they are not actively shunning students of different races, religions, and cultures. But it's easier for them to hang out with friends whose interests are more closely aligned with their own.

Take away the race and color part. Would the computer geeks want to hang out with the basketball team? The teens who favor preppy dress with those who prefer Goth? How likely is it to find kids who play in a rock or rap group choosing to spend Friday nights with members of the chess club?

During adolescence, young people search for their identity and try to answer important questions about who they are and where they are headed. They look for those answers by looking to people, young and old, whose backgrounds are similar to their own. This phenomenon is particularly noticeable in the African-American community. "For black youth, asking 'Who am I?' includes thinking about 'Who am I ethnically and/or racially? What does it mean to be black?' " says psychologist Beverly Daniel Tatum in her book *Why Are All the Black Kids Sitting Together in the Cafeteria?* To those who wonder why black students perhaps think more about race than white students, Tatum points out, "That is how the rest of the world thinks of them."

Yet, when you talk to adolescents, their view of future race relations is more positive. A similar ethnic background, they believe, is just one factor that may bring kids together. But different ethnic backgrounds do not necessarily have to keep kids apart. "By being with someone who is different, you learn about something new, whether it's food or a religious belief," says one sixteen-year-old girl. "After a while, always being with people who are like you is boring."

## Uncertainty, Doubts, Reservations, and Prejudices

Even parents who believe in tolerance and equality may find themselves feeling hypocritical when their daughter brings home a love interest whose background is different. If this experience has hit home, you are not alone. And questioning your daughter's choices does not necessarily mean you harbor racist thoughts. Examining your fears, however, may help you put them in perspective.

**You worry that your daughter will marry someone from a different culture.** You envision a wedding nightmare where the groom's family doesn't know a word of English. Slow down. In adolescence, both girls and boys explore who they are by learning about their peers. As the *USA Today* poll showed, most young people date outside of their ethnic group because they are attracted to someone or just plain curious. "I'm interested in Japanese language and culture," says one sixteen-year-old girl, whose parents are Puerto Rican. While she would like to date Asian boys, at this point her curiosity about the culture is driving that goal. When asked whether she would actually marry an Asian, she expressed doubts. "On holidays when the families get together, how would everyone talk?" she wonders. "His family would be on one side, mine on the other."

Rather than fast-forward to your daughter's wedding, keep your focus on the present. Look on her dating choices in a positive way. Learning about and appreciating differences is a valuable skill that will serve your daughter well in college, the workplace, and in relationships.

**You worry that your own culture will be lost.** Some parents worry about their customs and traditions dying out if their sons and daughters marry outside of their ethnic group. Some Asian-American groups, particularly Japanese-Americans, are concerned with losing their identity with so much cross-race marriage. Families who have recently come to the United States may feel they are fighting a losing battle. They may observe the old traditions at home, but their children go to school in a very Americanized culture. Will a daughter be tempted to break away by dating and ultimately marrying outside of her race?

Of course, that may happen. But there is a surprising statistic to consider. An estimated 60 percent of the world's weddings are arranged by family members or religious leaders. While most of these weddings occur outside the United States, many highly Americanized immigrants agree to these arranged pairings. In its March 10, 2003, issue, *New York Newsday* profiled Vibha Jasani, who graduated from Annadale High, in Virginia, and Virginia Tech, and then agreed to fly back to India so that her relatives could find her a husband. Even Vibha, who saw herself as independent, was shocked at her decision. In the end, she found it difficult to turn her back on her family's traditions.

Traditions need not be lost, however, no matter who your daughter ultimately chooses. In fact, the melding of two varied backgrounds can result in deeper appreciation and understanding by everyone involved. Sharing rituals, celebrations, and beliefs ensures that those special ceremonies endure.

**You accept as true the stereotypes of certain ethnic groups.** "My mom hates to see guys with their pants worn low and their underwear showing," says one fifteen-year-old. Somehow her mother equates this hip-hop/rap dress with drug use and violence. Oftentimes such nonflattering portraits of various groups are reinforced by what we see in the media or the opinions of others.

Some stereotypes go beyond dress to the heart of a person's ethnicity. In the wake of 9/11, many Arab Americans found themselves on the receiving end of anger and violence. "My parents tell me to watch out for certain races," says one girl, refusing to identify them, but hinting that they are to be feared.

Moving beyond entrenched opinion is never easy, particularly when it is driven by an event like 9/11. One book, however, offers a lesson on how that can be done. Warren Lehrer and Judith Sloan explored the new ethnic America by walking in their own backyard: the 112 square miles of Queens, New York, viewed as one of the most diverse areas of the United States. In their book, *Crossing the Blvd.: Strangers, Neighbors, Aliens in a New America,* they tell how five nights after the attack on the World Trade Center, four young Americans smashed an Egyptian coffee shop in the Astoria section of Queens. Even though the police caught the men, the owner refused to prosecute, saying he could understand their anger. Startled and chastised by his reaction, the men returned an hour later to help the owner clean up his store. The five talked well past dawn, with their anger turning to understanding, even forgiveness.

Breaking down stereotypes is never easy. It's hard work because it involves taking the time to learn about others firsthand, rather than accepting the judgment of someone else. Doing so, however, beginning in our own neighborhoods, can put to rest some of the stereotypes so that we are not handing them down to our children.

**You worry your daughter will encounter prejudice, even violence.** In December 2004, Broadway star Idina Menzel, who won a Tony for her portrayal of the green witch in *Wicked,* arrived at the Gershwin Theater under heavy guard. Menzel, who is white, is married to the actor Taye Diggs, who is black. The couple was forced to be cautious after receiving death threats from someone who was angry over their interracial marriage.

Unfortunately, some individuals react in violent ways when they encounter a biracial couple. You may never be able to predict when your daughter and her friend will confront such a situation, and adolescents are apt to underestimate the danger. Forewarned is forearmed. Make sure your daughter understands you are not criticizing her choice, but that safety is your concern. Review with her where she will go and who else will be with her. Make sure she understands what to do in case she and her friend run into trouble.

Even if she and her date avoid violence, they may still have to endure stares, whispers, giggles, and worse. If she and her date have been together only at school and your house, going public may be a shock to them. Reassure her that she has done nothing wrong. While many now accept biracial couples without a second glance, others are still offended. Discuss with her how she and her friend can cope with such prejudice. Discourage her from engaging in debates or arguments with anyone who taunts the couple. Any remark could spark violence. Better to walk away.

**You are worried about prejudice from the boy's family.** "My daughter dated a boy from a very close Hispanic family," says one white mother. "While she was very open to meeting his family, I could tell from what she told me that they were not comfortable with her. She was devastated when he broke up with her, and I believe the move was forced by his parents."

We are all at different places on the acceptance ladder, and it doesn't matter what our ethnic backgrounds are. Particularly if you have taught your daughter to be open to other people, it can be confusing to have someone reject her. Give her plenty of time to grieve. When the time is right, talk about what she learned from this experience. Bridging differences isn't an easy task. While you still want her to be open-minded, she may understand that such a relationship will take more time and patience than she had thought.

**You are worried she will marry someone of her ethnic background.** Some parents have a different viewpoint: they hope their daughters will not marry someone from their own culture. "My mom wouldn't want me to marry someone of my own ethnic background," says one sixteen-year-old. When asked why, she says she doesn't know.

Some Hispanic women see the machismo in the Hispanic culture as hindering their progress, while some mothers of African-American daughters perceive a lack of successful young black men.

If your marriage or relationship to someone of your own culture failed, perhaps you are falling victim to stereotypes, believing that your daughter should avoid making a similar mistake. Be honest. There are many other relationships that have succeeded, that brought together two people from your ethnic makeup. Try not to generalize. Encourage your daughter to judge people as individuals, not as representatives of their culture.

**You are worried about religious differences.** "I'm open to other religions," says one fifteen-year-old, who was raised a Catholic. "Some religions, however, aren't open to accepting others." Religious differences do present a challenge if a couple decides to marry. If your daughter encounters such a dilemma when she is older, hopefully she and her partner will be able to work out an arrangement whereby each will be afforded religious freedom and agreement will be reached on what beliefs will be handed down to any children that result from the union. While your daughter is merely dating, however, allow her to learn about other religions. Attending other religious celebrations will increase her awareness and benefit her in the long run.

## Multiethnic Adolescents— Straddling the Divide

Jasmine is biracial. Her father is African-American, her mother white. Most of her life Jasmine was asked the question "What are you?" People's scrutiny made her uncomfortable. Why, she wondered, are people so eager to categorize you? Her mother encouraged her to be herself and not feel compelled to answer people's questions. "Now," her mother says, "Jasmine is fifteen, old enough to date. I know boys and their parents will be asking those questions over and over again."

Jasmine has lots of company. A growing number of adolescents are biracial or multiracial, identifying themselves with more than one race. According to the 2000 U.S. Census, approximately 2.4 percent of the population, over 6.8 million Americans, identify with two or more races. Nearly half of that group—42 percent—like Jasmine, is under eighteen. That statistic has dramatic implications. No matter whom these young people end up marrying, their children will be multiracial. Projecting out into future, that group will continue to increase geometrically, with grandchildren, great-grandchildren, and so on, having more than one race as part of their identity.

Biracial and multiracial adolescents have a unique perspective on cross-race dating. After all, someone like Jasmine is herself the product of an interracial union. She has watched her parents manage their relationship, at times successfully, but sometimes not. She knows that no matter whom she dates or marries, she may face similar challenges.

However, she's a long way from marriage. While she is dipping her toe into the adolescent social pool, how can her parents help her prepare for some of the surprises that may lie ahead? Here are some ideas.

**"What are you?"** Jasmine's mother knows that her daughter will be faced with this question. While it's illegal to demand such information during a job interview, there are no such limitations placed on a boy's parents. Prepare your daughter to expect this query and encourage her to answer it in a way that makes her feel comfortable. Hopefully, the boy's parents will be considerate of her feelings and not probe.

**"You can't be both!"** Biracial students rant against those who force them to identify themselves with only one race. If a boy pressures your daughter to pick sides, you may want to ask her, in a nonconfrontational way, "Why is he being so insistent?" If he is of one race, does he think his parents and friends will be more accommodating of their relationship if she chooses a side? By trying to please and not offend anyone, she will sacrifice her own self-esteem and sense of identity. Encourage her to embrace all parts of her background. Help your child understand that the key to being welcomed by others is claiming her own unique identity and not giving in to society's or peers' expectations.

# INTERRACIAL DATING

**Advantages**

Interracial couples

- Are exposed to a wider range of cultural experiences.
- Learn about honesty and acceptance, two character-istics essential for success in school, college, the workplace, and in relationships.
- Develop more empathy for people of different races.

**Challenges**

Interracial couples

- May encounter anger, resentment, even violence from others.
- May have to choose which group to be with in so-cially segregated schools.
- May have to work harder to iron out differences re-lated to religion and traditions.

**Suggested Reading About Race and Racial Identity**

Chideya, Farai. *The Color of Our Future.* (New York: Mor-row, 1999). Chideya interviewed multiracial teens from all over the United States and adds her own in-terpretation and commentary.

Gaskins, Pearl Fuyo. *What Are You? Voices of Mixed-Race Young People.* (New York: Henry Holt, 1999). Gaskins conducts in-depth interviews with eighty mixed-race teens who speak openly about the challenges they face in dating, family life, and prejudice from all groups.

Guzman, Sandra. *The Latina's Bible: The Nueva Latina's Guide to Love, Spirituality, Family, and La Vida.* (New York: Three Rivers Press, 2002). Guzman talks to girls who feel torn between two worlds—the Latina culture and twenty-first-century America.

Nam, Vickie, ed. *Yell-Oh Girls! Emerging Voices Explore Culture, Identity, and Growing Up Asian American.* (New York: Perennial Currents, 2001). Young Asian-American girls talk frankly about what it's like to grow up in two very different cultures.

Nash, Gary. *Forbidden Love: The Secret History of Mixed-Race America.* (New York: Henry Holt, 1999). What do Thomas Jefferson, Pocahontas, and Phil Gramm have in common? *Forbidden Love* describes how all of these well-known Americans crossed racial lines in their relationships.

Tatum, Beverly Daniel, PhD. *Why Are All the Black Kids Sitting Together in the Cafeteria? And Other Conversations About Race.* (New York: Basic Books, 2003). Tatum explores self-segregation in college dining halls, faculty lounges, and corporate cafeterias. Her book can provide a focus for discussing the challenging issues surrounding race relations.

**Young Adult Novels with Multicultural Themes**

Crutcher, Chris. *Whale Talk.* (New York: Greenwillow, 2001).

Frank, E. R. *Life Is Funny.* (New York: Atheneum, 2002).

Nolan, Han. *Born Blue.* (New York: Harcourt, 2001).

Woodson, Jacqueline. *The House You Pass on the Way.* (New York: Delacorte, 1997).

———. *If You Come Softly.* (New York: Putnam, 1998).

**Free to choose.** At some point, your daughter may feel closer to one part of her ethnic background than another. In a few years, her opinion could flip again. Her dating choices may reflect her current state of mind. As long as you approve of the boy in other ways, allow her this dating freedom. Learning about the backgrounds of others is the way she will ultimately learn about her own.

## The Color of Love

If your daughter is dating someone of a different background, she may think she already knows everything possible to manage the relationship in a positive way. If they have not been outside the school environment, however, her information may be limited. She may need more help than she thinks. Remember, you are not trying to send your daughter down the aisle with this boy. But you do hope that when they part ways (and most likely they will) she will have an appreciation of his background and culture. Here are some things you can do.

**Encourage her to read.** If the boy's parents were born in another country, find out where and suggest that she go on the Internet and read about their country. Have her read a novel set in his culture or region of the world, for example *The Kite Runner* by Khaled Hosseini, set in Afghanistan. When she meets the boy's parents, she will be able to say something meaningful about their culture. Her courtesy will be remembered, and she will have learned something worthwhile.

**Talk about clothing.** In some cultures, especially Muslim, women dress conservatively or favor native dress. Indian women wear saris, for example. While the boy's parents may be accustomed to seeing pictures of half-clothed starlets and models in magazines and on TV, they might not be so eager to see their son date a scantily clad girl. Dressing properly will show them respect.

**Review customs.** Will she be expected to shake hands or bow? In some cultures looking someone straight in the eye, common in the United States, is considered rude. She should ask the boy if there is anything special she should or should not do when meeting his parents.

**Review the menu.** If your daughter will be eating at the boy's house, encourage her to at least try what is put in front of her. Good table manners should be de rigueur.

No matter what your fears are for your daughter as she meets and dates boys of different backgrounds, give her room to explore and grow. Keep in mind that the world we knew as adolescents is nothing like the world she lives in. Our prejudices, which grew out of our history, have no place in the environment she walks through today. Time has marched on. Much has been left behind and our fear of others who are different should be one of those things.

# CHAPTER 9

# The Girl Can't Help It

*Same-Sex Attractions—*
*More Puzzling for More Girls*

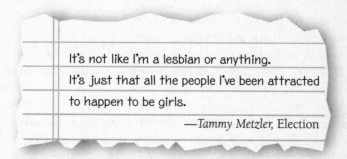

It's not like I'm a lesbian or anything.
It's just that all the people I've been attracted
to happen to be girls.

—*Tammy Metzler,* Election

"The only dance my daughter has been to at school was the one sponsored by the Gay/Straight Alliance," says the mother of Lindsay, fifteen. "She's always been very liberal, so I didn't think much about it at the time." But several other factors have caused Lindsay's mother to take notice. For example, Lindsay's last two boyfriends turned out to be gay. Now her mother is wondering, "Could my daughter be gay?"

Unlike Lindsay, your daughter may not openly question her own orientation. Don't think, however, that this issue won't touch her life. Adolescence is a tumultuous time for many kids, and figuring out sexual identity is a big piece of the puzzle. Right now, some of her closest friends may be struggling to find answers. With kids coming out at earlier ages, even in middle school, chances are your daughter may find herself caught up in one of her peer's sexual dramas. What happens, for example, when she dates a boy, and falls head over heels, only to discover that he's gay? She may have a best girlfriend who comes out. How will that news affect their relationship?

Lindsay, like all of our daughters, has grown up on a steady diet of fairy tales, movies, and romance novels where Prince Charming, or some modern version, captures the heroine's heart. This boy-girl story line is viewed as normal, widely acknowledged by society. Adolescent girls are supposed to swoon over male singers, athletes, movie stars, and other celebrities. Indeed, we named this book *Boy Crazy!* because the majority of adolescent girls are preoccupied with boys.

For a small minority of girls, however, that romantic scenario may seem too simplistic. If she is supposed to be attracted only to boys, why is she also attracted to girls? Her friends may be plastering their walls with photos of Usher, Leonardo DiCaprio, and Matt Damon, while she may find herself adding pinups of Ashlee Simpson, Beyoncé Knowles, and Britney Spears. Discovering she is different, during a time when adolescents strive so hard to fit in with a peer group, can be a frightening experience. How can a girl admit, to her peers and her parents, perhaps even to herself, that she may be a lesbian or bisexual?

Perhaps, like Lindsay's mom, you just have suspicions and haven't openly discussed the topic with your daughter. You may think, "Why does she always dress like a soccer player?" Maybe you look back and ponder that she never played with dolls, preferring her brother's cars and trucks. Once you may have celebrated her individuality and scoffed at stereotypes. Now, you wonder.

In the end, Lindsay's mom realized that her daughter merely felt confused. That happens more often than not. Still, your child (or a close friend of hers) may find herself in the gay minority. Your guidance can help her through this baffling time.

She may be filled with angst because she is attracted to her best friend. Or, she may think, "I'm always so uncomfortable around boys. Does that mean I'm gay?" This interval will be challenging for both you and your daughter and you will want to do whatever you can to help and support her.

Obviously, if you finally discover that your daughter is gay, you will want to seek out additional information. We will get you started, and at the end of this chapter, you will find a list of books to check out. In the interim, however, you may just need to keep an open mind while your daughter attempts to answer some very important questions. Rest assured that you are not alone.

## Gay. Lesbian. Bisexual. Transsexual. Transgender— Learning the Differences

During early adolescence, young people begin to explore their sexuality. Who are they attracted to and why? The question of sexual orientation occupies a great deal of their thinking. "Sexual orientation emerges for most people in early adolescence without any prior sexual experience," according to the American Psychological Association. Young people cannot help but be aware of society's expectations—being attracted to someone of the opposite sex. First sexual encounters often are heterosexual and may even be seen as serious. Your daughter may have a crush on a boy in middle school, even have a steady boyfriend in high school. Girls typically take a longer time than boys to think through their sexuality.

A 2004 study by the National Gay and Lesbian Task Force estimates that 3 to 6 percent of the nation's 15 million high school students may be gay or think they are gay. According to research done at a Minnesota public school, 11 percent of junior and senior high school students said they were "unsure" of their sexual orientation. Many more young people suspect they are gay, even engaging in same-sex activities, but are unwilling to identify themselves as homosexual.

"This disinclination of youth to say, 'I'm lesbian/gay' is in large part the result of the pervasive homophobia and hetero-sexism that characterizes their world," according to Ritch C. Savin-Williams, a clinical and developmental psychologist in the Department of Human Development at Cornell University. He notes that romantic relationships serve as an important developmental stepping stone for adolescents. Those whose true feelings are squelched by society's prejudices, however, miss out on this opportunity.

What does it mean to be gay? Being gay, the term mostly used for males, or lesbian, for females, means that a person's attraction on all levels—physical, emotional, romantic—is to someone of the same sex.

Someone who is bisexual is attracted to people of both sexes. Because adolescence is all about experimentation, some young people may explore both same-sex and opposite-sex relationships before finally discovering whether they are straight or gay. Others may ultimately conclude they are indeed bisexual.

Transsexuals are not necessarily gay. Transsexuals feel they were born in the wrong body. A boy feels he should have been a girl, while a girl longs to be in a boy's body. Some of these people may undergo sex-change operations later in life. Gay and lesbian people, on the other hand, do not feel trapped in the wrong gender, even though their ideas about men and women may fly in the face of traditional sex roles.

Transgenders, an emerging group now gaining prominence on many college campuses, may also be transsexual—changing their gender with the help of surgery or hormones—or they may simply defy being categorized as either male or female. The group has coined the term *gender queer* to set themselves apart. Several prestigious colleges, including Sarah Lawrence, Brown, Wesleyan, and Smith, now offer special accommodations (single-stall bathrooms and designated housing) for their transgender students.

## "That's So Gay!"

While colleges are working hard to make their environments more comfortable for gay students, middle and high schools remain hostile places. An adolescent needs incredible courage and strength not only to come out, but also to let friends know she is questioning her sexual orientation. According to a 2004 poll by the Gay, Lesbian, and Straight Education Network (GLSEN), antigay language is widespread in schools. Sixty-six percent of students report using homophobic language, such as "that's so gay," to describe something that is wrong, bad, or stupid. Eighty-one percent of students report hearing homophobic language in their schools frequently or often.

"It is probably shocking to adults how many of their children are using offensive homophobic language day in and day out in our nation's high schools," says Marty McGough, director for Widmeyer Research and Polling, which, along with Penn, Schoen, and Berland Associates, conducted the GLSEN poll of ninth- and twelfth-grade students across the country.

A 2003 National School Climate Survey found that four out of five lesbian, gay, bisexual, and transgender students report hearing homophobic remarks often in their schools and that 83 percent of the time faculty or staff don't intervene.

Creating a safe and nurturing school environment for openly gay and bisexual students is seen by many advocates as critical to the development and success of these young people.

Unfortunately, both middle and high schools have been slow to embrace programs to help gay students. A 2004 GLSEN report gave failing grades to forty-two states for their lack of attention to this group's special needs. The report summarized state laws that affect school environments for all students, particularly gay students. GLSEN found that only eight states and the District of Columbia had statewide legal protections for students based on sexual orientation.

"In classrooms where 'faggot' is heard more often than the pledge of allegiance and 39 percent of LGBT (lesbian, gay, bisexual, and transgender) students report being physically assaulted because of their sexual orientation, our schools and the states that govern them are failing," says GLSEN executive director Kevin Jennings.

## An Adolescent Group at Risk

A multitude of studies have found that gay youth are at risk for

**Suicide.** A report by the U.S. Department of Health and Human Services found that gay and lesbian youth are two to three times more likely to commit suicide than other youth. Thirty percent of young people who succeeded in killing themselves did so after grappling with their sexual identity. While only one in ten heterosexual teens attempts suicide, two out of every three gay or lesbian teens do so.

Do gay youth attempt suicide simply because of their sexual orientation, or are they driven to attempt suicide because of the societal issues they encounter, such as being shunned by family, friends, and support systems at school? Several studies in the United States and Canada lend credence to the latter explanation. One survey of 221 gay, lesbian, and bisexual youth in the United States and Canada found that more than 40 percent of those who had attempted suicide were having difficulties with family members, school, and peers.

**Homelessness.** Unfortunately, many young people who come out to their parents end up being kicked out of their homes. Experts estimate that 30 to 40 percent of runaways and homeless youths identify themselves as gay or lesbian.

**Substance abuse.** A 1995 study of 4,000 youths by the Massachusetts Department of Education found that gay kids were five times more likely to use cocaine than their straight peers.

**Violence.** Being gay often means becoming a target for physical abuse. The Massachusetts study found that gay, lesbian, or bisexual youth were seven times more likely than other kids to avoid school out of fear for their safety. A 1997 study by the Vermont Department of Health found that the gay kids were threatened or injured with a weapon three times more than kids who were straight.

**Failure in school.** Needless to say, worrying about whether someone will attack you, verbally or physically, creates a stressful school environment. No wonder that many gay and lesbian youth find themselves struggling in school. The drop-out rate for gay and lesbian youth is higher than for those who are straight.

**Sexually transmitted diseases, including AIDS.** Because of the way these diseases are spread, lesbians are less at risk than are their gay male counterparts.

## Keeping Communication Open

If you sense your daughter is wrestling with her sexual identity, how do you get her talking about such a sensitive topic? Avoid the blunt approach. Coming right out and asking, "Are you gay?" will ensure that she clams up, even if you ask the question in your most gentle voice.

Rhett Godfrey was a high school senior when he wrote *The Teen Code: How to Talk to Us About Sex, Drugs, and Everything Else—Teenagers Reveal What Works Best.* He went right to the source, gay teens, and asked how they wanted to be approached by their parents. According to Godfrey, teens suggested parents bring up the topic after watching a TV show that featured a gay character, perhaps an episode of *Will & Grace.* A parent should ask a child how she feels about the character and about homosexuality in general.

They turned thumbs down, however, on a parent saying, "You

know it's okay if you're gay." The teens felt this statement would be construed as an attempt to wrest a confession out of them. A better way? "You know I love you unconditionally—it wouldn't matter if you were gay, straight, or anything else for that matter."

Let's assume that your middle school daughter admits she is puzzled about her sexual orientation. Ask her what has happened to make her feel that way. You have to walk a delicate line here. You want to reassure her that perhaps some of her fears are unfounded. Yet if her feelings about homosexuality are strong, you don't want to send the message that you disapprove. Here are some sample conversations:

DAUGHTER: "I really like Miranda. I want to be with her 24/7. Am I gay?"

MOTHER: "Well, when you really like someone, you do want to spend a lot of time with that person because she makes you feel good. You and Miranda have always been good friends. But liking someone of the same sex doesn't always mean that you are gay."

DAUGHTER: "Mandy made fun of me because I don't have any dolls in my room, just sports stuff. She says I must be gay."

MOTHER: "Some athletic girls are gay, but some aren't. Martina Navratilova, the tennis champ, is, but Mia Hamm, the soccer star, is not. Being a good athlete doesn't mean you are automatically gay."

DAUGHTER: "All my guy friends are gay. Does that mean I am, too?"

MOTHER: "I know you like Mark and Sam because they are kind and funny. I'm happy they are your friends. But their sexual orientation doesn't affect yours. You are free to make up your own mind about that."

You get the idea. Offer reassurance, but don't offer negative opinions about homosexuality. After any of your conversations, make sure your daughter knows that you love her and always will, and that she should feel free to come and talk with you whenever she has questions.

## Coming Out at Younger Ages

Sarah was in middle school when she first began to feel different. Her after-school hours were filled with sports—soccer, hockey, track. She turned a deaf ear to her mother's pleas that she wear more feminine clothing, opting instead for football jerseys and T-shirts. While her girlfriends oohed and aahed over frilly lingerie from Victoria's Secret, she chose to wear gray sports bras and plain white Jockey underwear. She kept her hair short and brushed back and never wore makeup. Her only piece of jewelry was a heavy metal watch.

When she was thirteen and in the eighth grade, she had her first and last boyfriend, Alex, fifteen. They met on a two-week mountain biking trip. Their first sexual encounter (and Sarah's first sexual encounter ever) was fast and furious. They went further than she had ever thought she would. Their relationship, however, turned out to be long-distance and short-lived. She broke up with him because she recognized she had feelings for women but didn't know how to act on those feelings. She became angry at Alex, blaming him for causing her ambivalence. She thought she might be bisexual, but soon realized she was a lesbian, because she wasn't attracted to boys at all.

In fact, she was never comfortable with the physical aspect of a boy-girl relationship. Kissing Alex never felt right. When that realization struck, she began to understand that she had taken on a boyfriend not because she was attracted to him, but because as a teenage girl, that was what she was expected to do. If she was totally honest with herself, Sarah knew it was girls she was attracted to, not boys.

Shortly after, she was invited to a friend's birthday party in another city. Knowing she would be among young people she had never met before, she decided the event would be her coming-out party. Rather than the luscious dresses the other girls wore, Sarah showed up in black slacks, a white shirt, and heavy black shoes. She asked her friend to introduce her to everyone as "Seth." No one knew she was really Sarah.

Somehow that evening emboldened Sarah to unveil her new persona to family and friends. While her parents were shocked at first, they took the news surprisingly well. When Sarah asked to transfer to a more liberal boarding school from her staid private school, her parents readily agreed. Shortly after arriving at her school, she found herself attracted to another girl who also was gay. She happily e-mailed the news to one of her friends.

Sarah's experience, coming out at such a young age, is no longer unusual. Young people are more aware of their sexuality and are recognizing differences earlier. Depending upon their community and school environment, many young people are emboldened to declare their sexual orientation to others. Beyond that, they become involved in gay-oriented educational and political groups.

Many factors are responsible for young people coming out earlier and becoming more politically active in gender-based issues. These factors include:

**Increased public awareness.** More and more gay people are refusing to hide their sexual orientation. Familiarity with a gay person helps to break down barriers. According to a 2004 poll by the GLSEN, nearly three fourths of high school students know a gay or lesbian person, 48 percent know a lesbian or gay classmate, and 11 percent know a gay or lesbian teacher. Sixty-five percent of students identify their personal experiences with gay people as an important influence in their attitudes about gay people, according to the GLSEN survey.

**Media portrayals.** In the GLSEN survey, 28 percent of students acknowledged the important role played by the media. TV shows and movies that spotlight gay and lesbian persons in a positive way help to increase understanding and acceptance.

**Gay marriage and gay adoptions.** Seeing gay couples celebrating their partnerships through commitment ceremonies or, where legal, marriage, helps young people visualize a future. In addition, gay couples who have adopted or lesbians who have given birth through artificial insemination show young people they can have a family too.

**Advocacy groups.** Organizations for gays, their parents, and friends offer encouragement and support. Besides GLSEN, the National Gay and Lesbian Task Force, and Parents, Families, and Friends of Lesbians and Gays (PFLAGS), many local support groups have sprung up. Besides helping gays, these groups create a visible presence to inform and educate the public.

**Gay-straight alliances.** Schools that have set up groups to bring gay and straight students together help to increase awareness and tolerance schoolwide. For homosexuals, having their straight friends not only accept them but also work to make the school environment safer is a tremendous show of support and caring.

**Internet.** Gay associations on the Web that can distribute information, help students find local support groups, and even assist gays in meeting others socially have opened up a whole new world. Many students who once felt isolated now can reach out to others through cyberspace. Of course, as in all encounters on the Web, girls should avoid anonymous chat rooms, stick with those associated with reputable groups, and never agree to meet anyone they have met on the Internet alone in a strange place.

## Dealing with the News

When your daughter comes to you with the news that she is questioning her sexual identity, or that she has already decided that she is gay, you may initially have trouble understanding what she is going through. Your first thoughts are apt to bring your own fears and concerns to the surface.

**Where did we go wrong?** Even the best parents are apt to blame themselves for their child's ambivalence or homosexuality. A working mother might be thinking, "If only I had stayed at home," while the stay-at-home mother will be thinking, "If only I had a career I might not have smothered her so." Dads, too, might take off on a guilt trip: "I shouldn't have traveled so much." Or "Why did I encourage her to play so many sports?"

What shapes sexual orientation for most people, according to the American Psychological Association, is a complex series of interactions of biological, psychological, and social factors. You may have pushed your daughter to play soccer, but so have millions of other parents whose daughters are heterosexual.

In any event, looking back will prove to be neither insightful nor constructive. Rather than lamenting what you did or didn't do, look ahead to what you will do now that you know.

**What will people think?** While most of us are loathe to be honest about it, we do care what our friends and neighbors think. Learning your daughter is a lesbian is bound to make even the most liberal parent a little anxious. You worry for yourself, how your relatives and friends will react. But most of all, you worry for your daughter. Will her grandparents reject her? Will your siblings, her aunts and uncles, criticize her?

How you reveal the news to your relatives will greatly influence how they take the news. The more positive you can be, the less likely they will be negative. Remember, part of their concern will be for what this news has done to you. If you keep the focus on supporting your daughter, hopefully they will too.

**What will her life be like?** We all have hopes and aspirations for our children. Most likely, you want your daughter to complete her education, get a good job, have good friends, marry, and have children. The news that a daughter is a lesbian may seem to place those dreams in jeopardy. In reality, however, your daughter can still achieve all those things, if she wants to. If your child were heterosexual, that would still be no guarantee that the plans you laid out for her would come to fruition. Keep in mind that your daughter's sexual orientation is just one facet of her personality. She can still have a healthy, happy, fulfilled life, even if that life is different from the one you envisioned.

## How to Help Your Daughter

Most of us know very little about what it's like to be a gay person in what is, essentially, a straight society. You may have had little reason up to now to do research on the subject. With your daughter's news, you now have the best reason ever to educate yourself.

**Be thankful.** Many gay youth never tell their parents for fear they will be rejected. The fact that your daughter told you shows that she trusts you and values your relationship. Treasure that faith.

**Read.** There is no dearth of material. Begin with *Now That You Know: A Parent's Guide to Understanding Their Gay and Lesbian Children,* by Betty Fairchild and Nancy Hayward, two mothers who draw on their own experiences to give others insight and advice. A book that both you and your daughter can read is *Free Your Mind: The Book for Gay, Lesbian, and Bisexual Youth— And Their Allies,* by Ellen Bass and Kate Kaufman.

Don't stop with these two books, however. Books for the gay and lesbian communities now make up large sections in bookstores and are sold online by Amazon, Barnes & Noble, and others. Browse through and read some of the news of the reviews before making your choices. Besides nonfiction, particularly stories of coming out, there are many novels written by and for gays. (See our suggestions at the end of this chapter.)

**Surf the Web.** The Internet is the best vehicle for gathering information from many different sources. You can read newspaper and magazine articles, find support groups, and even chat with other parents going through the same experience.

**Listen.** The conversation you have with your daughter when she reveals her sexual orientation is only the beginning. You may be too stunned and overwhelmed at first to say much or ask many questions. Over the next few weeks and months, find the time to have many more talks. You may have tons of questions, but it's important to let your daughter do a lot of the talking. She has probably been holding this news in for a long time and, no doubt, will have much to say. Give her a safe environment to open up, without interrupting or appearing judgmental.

**Advocate.** There's a reason so many parents of gays wind up becoming activists. They soon see how unfair the world is for their children. You may never have had a reason before to intervene at school, camp, or with your daughter's sports team. But if you feel she has been treated unfairly because of her sexual orientation, you should protest. Once she comes out, she may be teased at school. Keep on top of the situation and don't be reluctant to seek out school administrators to voice your concerns.

If your school does not have a gay-straight alliance, push to have one established. Work through your parents' association. If your daughter has some friends she can enlist to push for the formation of this group, tell her she should do so.

Some gay children ultimately have no choice but to transfer to a school where the environment is more tolerant and caring. Gay support groups can help steer you toward such schools. Several cities now have schools where the majority of students are gay. While these schools have been controversial (some people feel segregating gay students only puts off the necessity of their dealing with the real world), advocates believe they help to protect adolescents during their most vulnerable formative years.

**Seek out role models.** Straight adolescents have many role models to choose from. It's more difficult for gay youth. Help your child to focus on finding gay role models, whether far-flung or in your community. A local support group may help you find women who could serve as mentors for your child. While you want to help your child adjust and cope, only someone who has been through the same situation can really relate.

**Advise patience with friends.** "One of the girls in my school told everyone she was gay and now no one will talk to her," one sixteen-year-old girl says. Help your daughter cope with some of the reactions she may receive from friends. Remind her that not all young people are open-minded, but that over time they may come around.

**Contact local gay organizations.** Many local support groups sponsor activities where gay and lesbian students can meet one another. Make sure that the group will attract others your daughter's age.

## Navigating the Dating Scene

For the young adolescent girl who thinks she may be gay, the dating scene can be excruciating. Not attracted to those she should be dating, she can't date those to whom she is attracted. Anticipating society's reaction, some young lesbians bury their feelings and attempt to fit in. They may feign interest in boys to appease and mislead their friends.

In general, the younger your child is when she comes out, the harder it will be for her. Let's face it. Middle school is still the place where the "cool group" rules the roost. And, chances are, none of those kids will be gay or if they are gay, they are most likely concealing their sexual orientation. Once your daughter tells you she is a lesbian, ask her whether she has told any of her friends. She may have selectively chosen a few close friends she felt she could trust to keep her secret and not reject her.

Explore with her whether she is comfortable with just you and a few friends knowing. Help her to understand that if she announces she is a lesbian to all her classmates, she may be letting herself in for a hard time. Yet if she is determined to do so, you should be there to support her.

Sooner or later, your daughter will meet someone special she wants to date. You may have thought you had accepted your daughter's news. Yet when you see her holding hands and even kissing another girl, you might find yourself back at square one. Give yourself time to adjust. Keep in mind that whether your daughter is heterosexual or lesbian, you are bound to be a little unsettled seeing her become a sexual being right before your eyes.

Depending upon your community, however, you might want to caution your daughter about overt displays of affection in public. Gays and lesbians have been targets of violence by homophobic individuals. In February 2004, Sakia Gunn, a fifteen-year-old sophomore from Newark, New Jersey, was stabbed to death when she spurned a man's advances, telling him she was gay. You don't want your daughter to become a statistic. Advise her to use her best judgment.

## "But I Thought He Liked Me!"

Finding out that her boyfriend is gay can throw an adolescent girl into a tailspin. Lindsay's mother actually wondered if the fact that her daughter's only two boyfriends were gay played a factor in her daughter's questioning her own sexual orientation.

Lindsay, however, is not alone. With more boys coming out, other adolescent girls are encountering this issue. Katie, fifteen, was attracted to Zack, also fifteen, the first time she met him. "He was cute and a really good guy," she says. "He told me he was attracted to me." Actions spoke louder than words. Katie says that Zack was her first hookup and was obviously turned on when they were together.

After they had been dating for several months, Katie was puzzled when Zack began to withdraw from her. He seemed angry and upset and she couldn't figure out why. Confiding in a friend, she was taken aback when she was told, "Katie, he's gay."

When Katie asked Zack about his sexual orientation, he told her he was bisexual. "I was shocked," Katie says. "It doesn't matter how gay-friendly you are, anytime your boyfriend tells you he's gay or bi, you're not prepared for it."

Even after hearing his news, Katie agreed to continue to date Zack. Soon, however, he broke it off. Katie remembers running home in tears.

Looking back, she realizes there were warning signs that she refused to recognize. "Pretty much everyone thought he was gay because of the way he acted and spoke," Katie says. While her friends' comments gave her pause, Katie kept an open mind. "It's hard to tell if someone is gay just because of the way they talk or act," she says. "I was on the fence. When I talked with him, I didn't get that vibe. And, of course, he wouldn't admit it."

Following the breakup, Katie says that Zack wouldn't talk with her. His sexual encounter with her triggered his doubts about his own sexual orientation. He couldn't separate what he was going through from his relationship with Katie, somehow blaming her for his dilemma. At the time, Katie found his anger hard to take. Now, however, she understands and offers advice to any girl who finds herself in a similar situation. "If a girl says she feels guilty, she shouldn't," Katie says. "Sooner or later, he was going to have to deal with his sexual orientation. If he's angry at you because he's gay, let him calm down." She and Zack are once again friends.

Katie's experience is no longer unusual. In fact, Katie says that one of her best friends dated a boy for several months, and "went pretty far," before finding out he was gay. At the time, both Katie and her friend were puzzled that their boyfriends could be so attracted to them and yet still be gay. Katie, now seventeen, looks back on the encounters and observes, "A teenage boy is dealing with raunchy hormones. He's at the sexual peak of his life. It doesn't matter if you're male or female, just that you're a body."

Claire's story is becoming a familiar one, too. Her best friend, Danielle, told her she was a lesbian. Claire was shocked at first, but soon realized she had failed to recognize some signs. "I don't believe in the stereotype that lesbians take on boy-girl parts in a relationship," says Claire. "But in Danielle's case, she is really 'butch,' always dressing like a boy and playing down any femininity. She really is not comfortable being a girl."

During adolescence, it's possible that your daughter, like Katie or Claire, could be caught up in a friend's experimentation. How can you help your daughter through these times? Here are some suggestions:

**Don't criticize the friend or boyfriend.** Help explain to your daughter what her friend is going through. While she may feel hurt over the events that have transpired, explain that her friend is having a difficult time and may need some space to sort out his or her feelings. At some time in the future, your daughter will probably once again be friends with this person. Anything negative you say may damage your relationship.

**Discuss sexual orientation.** When she has had time to calm down, ask her if she has any questions. You may want to talk about your own experience, how you determined your own sexual orientation.

**Emphasize the value of friendship.** If your daughter's friend has recently come out, he or she may be facing a hard time at school and among peers. Standing by someone is a true test of friendship. Doing so won't be easy for your daughter, but give her your support and encourage her to do so.

Do you remember how you first sorted out questions about your own sexual orientation? One mother remembers:

I was in the fifth grade and had a huge crush on a sixth-grade girl named Sherry. I used to sit in class and doodle her name all over my books. I had such strong feelings for her, and worried that there was something wrong with me. Could I discuss what was happening with my mother? Never! I suffered in silence, until Sherry moved to a new school and I finally discovered boys. I want to make sure my daughter never goes through such torture. Whether she's gay, straight, or just confused, I want her to know I'm here for her. And you bet I'll tell her about Sherry.

The new millennium is shaping up as a time when we appreciate and celebrate differences, whether those variations relate to race or sexual orientation. Your daughter will be taking her cues from you. Keeping your language free of homophobic observations will impress her. If you had an experience like the mother above, tell your daughter about it. She will know she can talk with you and that you will be there to help and support her, no matter how she answers the question about her sexual orientation.

## Resources

Help your daughter appreciate gays and lesbians who have made a significant contribution to society. You can find books about the following individuals: Leonardo da Vinci, mathematician Alan Turin, Willa Cather, Socrates, Marcel Proust, Virginia Woolf, Herman Melville, Pyotr Ilich Tchaikovsky, Frida Kahlo, and James Baldwin.

Gay and lesbian-themed books include:

*From the Notebooks of Melanin Sun* by Jacqueline Woodson
*Am I Blue? Coming Out from Silence* by Marion Dane Bauer
*Two Teenagers in Twenty: Writing by Gay and Lesbian Youth* by Ann Heron
*Families: A Celebration of Diversity, Commitment, and Love* by Aylette Jenness and Michele Paulse
*The Shared Heart: Portraits and Stories Celebrating Lesbian, Gay, and Bisexual Young People* by Adam Mastoon

# CHAPTER 10

# You've Got Mail

## Romance Online

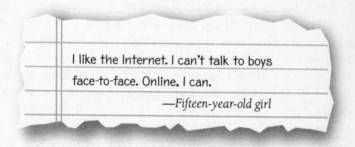

> I like the Internet. I can't talk to boys
> face-to-face. Online, I can.
>
> —*Fifteen-year-old girl*

Since the beginning of the school year, Jessica has harbored a secret crush on Todd, one of the "hottest" boys in the eighth grade. Although she sits across from him in history class, Jessica might as well be invisible. Todd never looks her way. At lunchtime, he is surrounded with his numerous friends, both boys and girls, laughing, playing music, passing around their cell phones.

"Go and talk to him!" urges her best friend, Kristen. But Jessica is painfully shy and just the thought of talking to Todd paralyzes her with fear.

"If you two talked, you'd hit it off," Kristen persists. "You both play the piano, love to ski, and never miss a hockey game on TV."

Jessica is impressed with her friend's inside information. "I know, I know!" she laments. "I even know that we both are dying to go to Australia." Yet crossing the school cafeteria seems as impossible as making it to the land down under. Nothing is more painful than an unrequited adolescent crush.

That evening, however, the impossible happens. Signing on to her computer, Jessica receives an instant message (IM) from Kristen.

KrisKross: T's scrn nm is FunDwnUndr. IM him now!

Jessica hesitates for only a minute before typing an IM to Todd: "Lik yr scrn nm. r u Aussie? I want 2 go."

Todd IMs back, "Not Aussie, but want 2 go 2."

Soon, the conversation that never happened in school is happening online. And Kristen was right. Her friend and Todd have a lot in common and a lot to talk about. Over a long holiday weekend, the IMs and e-mails fly back and forth. By the time they return to school, Todd is eager to talk with Jessica in person.

Some things haven't changed since you were a teen. It's still hard to face someone you like, talk to him, and hope he'll ask you out. Years ago, kids passed notes or used an intermediary to carry the message. These days, adolescents use the Internet. Hiding behind the blue screen, kids find it easier to talk. Modern-day pen pals can exchange opinions on music, trade jokes, and help each other with homework. Like Jessica, many boys and girls too shy to approach the opposite sex in person find it easy to talk online.

Cyberspace adds a new dimension to youthful romance. And young adolescents have embraced this new technology with relish. In addition to canoodling online, young people are using their cell phones, digital cameras, and video cameras to hasten the dating game.

The cyber approach to relationships has advantages. In a 2003 *Parade* survey, 56 percent of the boys and 79 percent of the girls said that the first thing that catches the attention of the opposite sex was looks. In cyberspace looks sometimes become secondary. Young people have the opportunity to judge someone they might never be attracted to in person using factors other than good looks—personality, sense of humor, empathy, intelligence.

But if young adolescents are comfortable with all these gadgets, their parents watch this new dating game with anxiety and fear. "Who is my daughter *really* talking to online? Is he a teenager or a pedophile?" Even if parents know the boy, they are probably not confident that all this romantic involvement over cable and phone lines is positive. While many a romance has blossomed in the electronic garden, problems also have sprung up like weeds. The potential for misuse by ill-intentioned and, sometimes, ill-informed young people looms large.

In this chapter, we will cover the Web—the good, the bad, and, sometimes, the ugly. We will give parents the information they need to supervise their daughters online. Yes, e-socializing can be dangerous in certain situations, but it also has a great deal to offer. If you are in doubt, we will reassure you. And if you are worried, we will give you strategies to keep your daughter safe.

Innovation often encounters resistance from the older crowd accustomed to doing business as usual. In fact, the Internet has been available to the public only since 1989. Young and older adolescents have never known a world without the Web and instant messaging. Adults take a longer time to adjust. There's no turning back the tide, however. The wise parent will become cyber savvy and learn how to help a daughter who, for better or worse, looks for love online.

## Learning About Love Online

Ask your daughter what she uses the Internet for, and she is apt to answer, "research." Glance at the screen when she is online and you will receive confirmation. She's looking at an encyclopedia page on the red-tailed hawk for a science project on threatened species. Yet, step out of the room, and her screen will zero in on a more interesting organism—the teenage boy, specifically the one with the killer smile and confident swagger who caught her eye at the basketball game on Saturday.

Yes, adolescents use the Internet for research. But, increasingly, what they research is the opposite sex. Sure, girls still pore over the pages of teen magazines, but there is such a wealth of information online, and the interactive quality of the Internet makes it even more exciting.

The Internet, still in its infancy, is rapidly growing in its influence. Nine percent of eight- to eighteen-year-olds gather their information about love and relationships from websites, 7 percent from chat rooms. The percentages increase with the age of the child. While only 4 percent of eight- to twelve-year-olds rely on those electronic sources, 13 percent of adolescents ages thirteen to eighteen learn about love on websites, 10 percent in chat rooms.

During the early phase of adolescent development, most of the IMing and e-mailing will be girl-to-girl, passing along gossip and talking about schoolwork. By phase two, girls are still talking, mostly to each other, but now the hot topic is hot boys. By the end of phase two and into the beginning of phase three, the boys are finally on board, and the conversations that fly across the screen are boy-to-girl. By phase four, a boy and girl could spend many hours talking online, as much time as their parents spent on the phone when they were teenagers. The technology may have changed, but the romantic objectives remain the same.

In 2002, the Youth Internet Safety Survey used telephone surveys to gather information from 1,501 young people, ages ten through seventeen. The survey found that 14 percent of young people developed close friendships online, 7 percent had face-to-face meetings with people they met online, and 2 percent developed romantic relationships through the Internet. While these percentages may seem low, researchers who have focused their work in this area see steady growth. "Given the extent of the Internet use among young people in the age categories covered by this survey, and given adolescents' natural interest in forming close relationships, the number of youths involved in close online friendships, romantic relationships, and face-to-face meetings with online friends is quite large and likely to increase as Internet use grows," says David Finkelhor, in his paper, "Close Online Relationships in a National Sample of Adolescents," reported in the *Journal of Adolescence.*

Talk to adolescent girls, and they back up Finkelhor's theory. "You hear kids say, 'what time are you going to be on? Okay, I will, too,'" one fifteen-year-old girl reports. Rather than meeting at the mall or the deli, young people congregate in cyberspace.

Of course, you can keep an eye on your teen when she is with friends at the mall or deli: Tracking her on the Web is more of a challenge. So start by doing some of your own homework on the complexities of the Internet, as well as the capabilities of new technology.

## Finding Your Way in Cyberspace

If you are like most adults, you use the Internet to check your e-mail, make hotel and air reservations, find directions on Map Quest, and shop for Christmas and birthday gifts. The more adventurous among us may IM our friends, download music, enter a bid on eBay, and occasionally visit a chat room on a topic that we find interesting.

Our kids do all those things—and more.

**E-mails.** Depending upon your job, you may receive a few or hundreds of e-mails a day. Most are probably business-related, some are from relatives and friends, others are solicitations and spam—junk e-mails. If you are like most adults, you regard e-mail as a necessary evil. You may not like it, but you know your business associates and clients prefer this means of communication.

Adolescents, on the other hand, *love* e-mail. They rush home from school to check their in-box. Just to hear that mechanical AOL voice announce, "You've got mail!" is music to their ears. And teens don't just send an e-mail to one person. Using their "buddy lists," with the screen names of dozens of their closest (and not so close) friends, they often beam their messages to large audiences.

**Instant Messaging.** This online function allows you to carry on a conversation with another person in real time. "I can only manage one IM conversation at a time," says one mother. "My daughter? She can talk to ten people at once. I don't know how she can keep track of so many conversations simultaneously."

IMs have nearly replaced the phone. And some young adolescents believe it has advantages. "Online, you have time to think about what to say," according to one fifteen-year-old girl. And these conversations can be as detailed and long-winded as the phone marathons we remember from our own teenage years. "I talk to one of my guy friends online and he sends really long IMs," one girl says.

**Web logs (blogs).** As a teenage girl, you probably filled page after page in your diary with intimate thoughts about your so-called life. Girls still like to journal and some do it by putting pen to paper. Increasingly, however, girls are musing about their lives and loves online. These web logs, or "blogs," are not kept under lock and key, but are put up on the Web for classmates to read. Because so much of what teen girls write about in diaries, and now in blogs, concerns love and romance, these writings can make for some steamy reading indeed.

**Websites.** Adolescents have any number of favorite websites they like to visit, often coinciding with a special interest. Young people like to share their special places, so it's possible your daughter and her friends are frequenting the same cyber-places. No doubt some of these websites deal with love, romance, relationships, and, inevitably, sex. Chances are that question about sex your daughter is too embarrassed to ask you may be answered after she does some research online.

**Chat rooms.** Chats are like electronic conference calls, with many different people participating at once. Adolescents can set up their own chat rooms, inviting just certain friends, or they can go to a public chat room on a website and talk with total strangers. Parents need to caution their young adolescents about talking with total strangers online or giving out personal information. Yet most young people report talking with other young people on these sites. And face-to-face meetings are a rarity. For teens, talking in a chat room to another teen is like having an electronic pen pal.

**Cell phones.** With plans coming down in price and parents worried about safety, most adolescents now own cell phones. Yet safety is probably the last thing on your daughter's mind when she turns on her cell phone. That device is her lifeline to her social world. Being able to send text messages, photos, and short videos to her friends just adds to the appeal.

**Camcorders.** When video cameras first came out, consumers used them to record baby's first steps, Mary's Sweet Sixteen, and mom and pop's anniversary party. A small group could gather around the set to watch the tape. Teens are into video-taping, too. But their audiences are vastly larger. The reason? Those videos can now be uploaded to a computer and placed on the Web. Now millions of people all over the world can watch the action your daughter taped at her last party.

Who knows what new device will find its way onto the marketplace—and into your daughter's hands—in the near future? We can only guess. What we do know, however, is that all this new technology is coming together—computers, phones, TVs—making communication faster, easier, and more far-reaching than ever before. Wireless technology, WiFi, already in use, means that young people no longer need to be "plugged in" to plug into their groups. That trend will accelerate, with more and more devices being able to wander free. The gadgets will become smaller and less expensive, thus opening the way for more families—and their children—to afford them. While our business lives will be affected, so will our family lives. We may not learn to master each new tool that comes along, but we should know enough so that we can help our children use new technology in a positive way.

## Love, Technology-Style

So how does all this new technology affect our daughters' social lives? What is being made more possible today that eluded us yesterday? Here are some of the scenes unfolding before parental eyes:

**Get me rewrite!** Rebecca is online talking to Adam, a boy from her class. She has never spoken to him before, although she has noticed him. When she asked her friends about him, they were of one opinion: "Cute, but no personality." Actually, Adam does have a personality, but when he is around girls his mind goes blank and the best he can do is stutter. Online, he suddenly takes on a new persona. No wonder! Adam has enlisted his very own Cyrano, his best friend, Brian, to help him out. With Brian on the phone, Adam relays his conversation with Rebecca. And clever, witty Brian whispers in Adam's ear the bon mots sure to land the heart of an adolescent girl. Before too long, Rebecca is enthralled. Adam isn't boring at all.

If this scenario seems like something out of a novel, it is! But it's also a true story in the lives of many adolescents. Editing themselves beforehand, sometimes with the help of a skilled writer, even the most tongue-tied young person can be savvy and articulate. And boys aren't the only ones looking for a scriptwriter. One girl says: "With the Internet, you can have a friend on the phone and say, 'Here's what I want to say. How do I say it?' And she can help!" Will this online love-dance actually turn into a face-to-face date or relationship? Perhaps. Or maybe Rebecca will fall for the true voice behind the screen, Brian. After all, Roxanne did.

**Reach out and touch someone.** Brenda met Claude through her friend, Amanda. Claude's parents and Amanda's parents had been friends most of their lives. While Claude and Amanda were close, they felt more brother and sister than boyfriend and girlfriend. Claude and Amanda were chatting online one day when Brenda IMed Amanda. Suddenly Amanda was struck with a thought. Why not introduce Brenda to Claude? Amanda gave Claude Brenda's screen name and told him to contact her.

Amanda was right. Claude and Brenda did hit it off, talking online just about every night. Claude lived in Montreal, Brenda in San Francisco. Learning about each other's countries, cities, schools, hobbies, friends, pets, consumed hours of online time. When Brenda had to do a history project researching a city, she chose Montreal and Claude happily e-mailed her information, websites, and his own personal thoughts about his city.

Summer vacation soon rolled around and Claude's family planned a trip to San Francisco to visit Amanda and her family. Brenda was thrilled. At last she would get to meet her online pen pal. Brenda and her parents were invited out to dinner with both families. Even though Brenda and Claude thought they knew each other well, their face-to-face meeting was awkward. Yet, by the end of the evening, they were talking without the aid of a computer.

Brenda and Claude managed some alone time, which included some hand-holding and a few kisses. They were now officially "going out."

Their long-distance relationship continued once Claude went back to Canada. But soon Brenda realized dating someone clear across the country, even though they talked every day, left much to be desired. When she suggested to Claude that they be just friends, he seemed relieved, too.

Brenda and Claude's experience is becoming more commonplace. According to the Youth Internet Safety Survey, 70 percent of young people who reported having a close Internet relationship with someone later corresponded by mail or telephone. Forty-one percent reported face-to-face meetings with their online friends. Almost all of these meetings—83 percent—involved youths who were within one year of age of each other. Only one, according to the survey, involved an adult who was more than five years older. (Surprisingly, that relationship was between a seventeen-year-old boy and a twenty-nine-year-old woman. The boy broke it off when he discovered the woman was married.)

The survey made another observation. Most of the close online relationships that resulted in face-to-face meetings were initiated when the parties were introduced by family or friends, just like with Brenda and Claude. And 60 percent of the youths said they told a parent before they met the person. Others told a friend. However, 10 percent told no one, which could be a cause for concern.

Yet take heart if your daughter seems to be losing her heart to someone far away. She may meet him, she may not. But chances are, she will learn something from this long-distance friendship.

**Casting a wider electronic net.** Girls in single-sex schools have limited ways to meet boys. "If it wasn't for the Internet, I would never meet any boys," says one sixteen-year-old who goes to an all-girls Catholic school. "Even if you go to coed dances, it's hard to keep up regular contact with the boys you meet."

The Internet, however, has changed all that. Now at coed dances, kids exchange e-mail addresses. In the days and weeks that follow, the e-mails fly back and forth. While dating may be the result, sometimes good friendships form instead. "One of my best friends is Max and I would never have met him if it wasn't for the Internet," says one girl.

Even students in coed schools benefit from this cross-school correspondence. Especially if your daughter's school is small, she may soon want to meet new people. Finding friends who live cross town may help her widen her social circle.

**Not ready for prime time.** Anne was in the sixth grade when she first began to think she might be a lesbian. Afraid to reveal her secret to anyone at home or school, she felt alone and isolated. When she was thirteen, she found a website sponsored by the Gay, Lesbian, and Straight Education Network. She was able to talk with other young adolescents, girls and boys, going through the same experience.

Should she come out? How would her parents react? Whom could she trust? The young people told her their stories and she was able to make a plan of action. She also found a social group a short bus ride from her house. There she was able to meet in person other gay adolescents and realize that she could have a social life.

For many gay adolescents like Anne, the Internet has proved to be invaluable. Besides the information she collected, she also gathered e-mails of friends and, eventually, a girl she decided to date.

**Text me.** Cell phones have given adolescents a versatile tool to keep in touch. Consider the case of Laurie, an eighth-grader. For several months, she has been dating Tommy, a boy in another town, someone she met through a friend. Her parents will allow her to see Tommy only on the weekend. "It's hard to get to know someone when you only see them once a week," sighs Laurie. During the week, however, Laurie and Tommy make use of technology. They send text messages to each other over their cell phones several times each day. "You can really get to know someone when you are constantly text-messaging each other," she says. "Otherwise, seeing him just one day a week, I would hardly know him and feel uncomfortable."

**"Some privacy, please!"** Adolescents, as you know, crave privacy. The child who once gave you unfettered access to her room now demands that you knock and wait until you hear "Come in!" before entering. (For more information on adolescents and privacy, see our book *What Are You Doing in There? Balancing Your Need to Know with Your Adolescent's Need to Grow.*) Diana, fifteen, was one teen who longed for privacy, not only from her parents, but also from her little brother, Dennis, eight. Every time Diana got on the telephone with a boy, Dennis would pick up an extension with the sole purpose of embarrassing her. Sometimes he would bark; other times he would shout until Diana was forced to either terminate her phone call or threaten to terminate her brother—or both!

Getting a cell phone was the answer to Diana's dreams. Now whenever her phone rang, she knew she could talk in complete privacy. No one was on an extension eavesdropping. Dennis, of course, would soon find other ways to torment Diana. After all, what are little brothers for? But at least on one front, Diana had found a refuge.

As you can see from the above examples, the basic goals of dating, to meet someone interesting, have not changed. But young people now have a wider variety of items at their disposal to help them accomplish that goal. If you find yourself concerned about how your daughter is meeting boys, try to separate the technology from your fears. Would you be as upset if your daughter were just using the home phone or sending love letters? If your daughter's boy crazy behavior alone has you concerned, have a talk with her. On the other hand, if you are bothered by the manner in which she is using electronic devices, that's another story. The potential for misuse does exist. And when you sense trouble, you need to step in.

## Sex, Lies, and Videotapes

An eighth-grade girl at a private school in New York City decided she was going to impress a boy she liked. Using a videocamera, she taped herself masturbating with a cleaning instrument. She sent the video, via e-mail, to the boy.

She got his attention. He wasted no time e-mailing the video to dozens of other adolescents. Within days it was hard to find a private school student in New York who hadn't seen the video or, at least, heard about it. Ultimately, the school was forced to deal with the ensuing scandal, giving out lectures and punishments.

Adults who hear this story are justifiably horrified and baffled. Why would a girl do such a thing? Didn't she comprehend what might happen to her and her reputation?

Chances are this girl's parents taught the girl how to use the camera and her computer, but never cautioned her about misuse. And there is a youth culture issue here. While we may regard her actions as scandalous, an adolescent might think, "What's so bad about that?" The last young woman to find her X-rated video being played on computers coast-to-coast was Paris Hilton. Was she censored and drummed out of public life? Hardly! Our celebrity-driven culture instead rewarded her with high ratings for her TV show, endorsement deals for everything from cell phones to jeans, and numerous covers on fashion and fan magazines.

This incident is not the only one in which adolescents have misused new technology with hurtful and, sometimes, disastrous results:

- David Knight was surprised—and alarmed—to find out that he was the subject of a page on the Internet, "Welcome to the web site that makes fun of David Knight." The site was filled with derogatory comments directed at David and his family. Among other accusations, David was portrayed as a pedophile using the date rape drug on young boys.

- A middle school girl took a trip to Toronto and found no one would talk to her when she returned to classes. Someone had started a rumor by using text messaging on cell phones that she had caught SARS (severe acute respiratory syndrome) while traveling.
- An overweight boy in Japan changing clothes in a school locker room didn't know he was being secretly photographed by a classmate using a picture phone. The embarrassing photos were soon posted on the Internet and sent to many of his classmates.
- Two high school girls had too much to drink at a party held in an upscale town in Westchester County. Cheered on by several boys, the girls began to kiss and fondle each other. One of the boys recorded the exploits on videotape, which soon was viewed by many of the students at the high school.

This activity has a new name—cyberbullying, using new communication technology to tease and torment others. Cyberbullies are taking humiliation to a frightening level. Hiding behind the anonymity of the Internet, cyberbullies are able to hurl around threats, spread rumors, trash reputations, and damage fragile egos, usually without being caught. The incredible scope of the Internet means that a cyberbully can reach millions with the click of a mouse. "Rather than just some people, say thirty in a cafeteria, hearing them all yell insults at you, [the web page] is up there for 6 billion people to see," David Knight told a Canadian TV reporter. "You can't get away from it."

Some cyberbullies are hard core. They have been bullying for years, using their mouths and fists to threaten others. Other cyberbullies are otherwise okay kids who somehow can't resist the temptation to pass along a hurtful rumor or send a nasty e-mail. At one talk we did, we asked middle schoolers how many of them had been harassed online. Virtually everyone raised his or her hand. More telling was when we asked how many had been the tormentor. Again, just about every student in attendance.

Parents, who foot the bill for their children's electronic toys, many times remain oblivious of the dangers for misuse. According to a 2000 study by the University of New Hampshire's Crimes Against Children Research Center, one in seventeen kids ages ten to seventeen had been threatened online and about one third of those found the incidents very upsetting. Another study done in 2002 in Great Britain by NCH, a children's charity, said that one in four students had been bullied online.

In the past, experts were most concerned about adults threatening children online. Now, however, an increasing number of complaints involve kids menacing their schoolmates. At no time do adolescent hormones and emotions run higher than when kids are thinking about that special person. When your daughter goes looking for love online, she could find heartache and trouble instead.

In the beginning of this chapter, we reviewed how adolescents use their computers, cell phones, and video cameras in positive ways to connect with others. Here are tales of the brokenhearted brought to you by new technology:

**How do I love thee?** Your daughter could pour her heart out to a boy she likes and soon find herself not counting the ways he likes her, but counting how many of her classmates have also read her private thoughts. E-mails can be forwarded to dozens, hundreds, even thousands of people. Adolescents, however, are trusting. And they don't understand the far-reaching aspects of cyberspace. Bring your daughter back to earth.

**Breaking up is hard to do—not!!** Telling someone it's over has never been easy—until now. "Hey, I don't want to go out with you anymore. C ya!" Cyber-cowards now have a new way to call it quits. Whether sent in an e-mail or IM, the offending party can avoid a face-to-face. If your daughter wants to break it off, at least encourage her to pick up the phone. If she's on the receiving end of the old heave-ho, be ready to console her.

**Rumor control.** Adolescents have never had any trouble spreading rumors. Now, however, with new technology, hurtful rumors can find their way to a wider audience. For an adolescent girl, a rumor directed at her sexual life can be devastating. Most times, these tales are untrue, but they take on a life of their own.

**"She's a lesbian!"** "I had a friend who had a rumor spread about her by her own brother," says one sixteen-year-old girl. Using his sister's screen name, he "confessed" to one of his sister's friends that she was gay. "He sent it to a lot of people and pretty soon it was all over school."

Unfortunately, the rumor that an adolescent is gay is still seen as the most harmful accusation that can be made. If the girl is not gay, she will have difficulty refuting the lie. And if she is gay and has not yet come out to family and friends having her secret "outed" before she is comfortable telling people may send her into a tailspin.

**Mistaken identity.** Adolescents are casual about letting friends know their passwords and use their screen names. Assuming a classmate's identity online, however, can result in confusion and catastrophe. A girl, thinking she is talking to a girlfriend about a boy in her class, may actually be talking to that boy. What she says was never meant for his ears and may hurt his feelings. Later on, if she discovered what happened, she might be angry at him and her girlfriend for tricking her.

**The Kodak moment.** Many more cell phones are being sold with picture phone capability. And adolescents are eagerly snapping away. As the boy from Japan discovered, these pictures can be taken when least expected. And, unlike those snapshots from the past, these can be uploaded to the Internet and sent out to a large audience. Warn your daughter about the potential for her to be "snapped." And think twice about outfitting her with equipment she may not need.

**The transformation.** In California, after a girl broke up with a boy, he created a website to make fun of her, morphed photos of her, and called her ugly names.

**Public vs. private.** Young adolescents need help drawing the line between what can be made public and what should remain private. Many girls use their web logs, "blogs," to record intimate details of their sexual lives. "I have an online diary and I have met some people over the Internet," says one girl. "One freaked me out because, after reading my diary, he started to talk dirty. I signed off and blocked his screen name."

Later on in life, your daughter may indeed become a writer and be driven to write her no-holds-barred memoir. But an adolescent who puts too much out there runs the risk of her peers or others using this information against her.

**Hitting the wrong note.** "Talking on the Internet is a problem because you never know the tone of the person's voice," says one fifteen-year-old. "They can say one thing and you can take it another way." Before your daughter overreacts to something she reads from a friend, tell her to talk to the friend in person.

## Hiding Behind the Screen

Since the dawn of time, the world of adolescent love has been fraught with anxiety. There were always ways for teens to hurt one another and harm reputations. A whispered rumor, a scathing remark passed in a note, an anonymous phone call in the night. How many of us have been on the receiving—or the giving—end of such acts?

The environment has changed for our children, however,

with the advent of the Internet and other technology. A note that was once passed to three people before the teacher intercepted it now can find its way around the world. And a teacher will have no way to stop it.

Adolescents can hide behind anonymity, covering their tracks by using multiple screen names. Even the most skilled technician will have to work long and hard to trace the source of a rumor. Kids feel free to do things online that they would never do in person. A boy breaking up with a girl via e-mail doesn't have to see her tears. Looking at his computer screen, he might as well be ordering a pair of jeans from the Gap.

Because cyberbullying and the misuse of the Internet are such new phenomena, school and law enforcement officials in the United States and other countries are still sorting out the legal technicalities. "Most of what is done online is protected as free speech," says Frannie Wellings, policy fellow, Electronic Privacy Information Center, Washington, DC.

In contrast to print publications, where individual stories are checked for libel and accuracy, the atmosphere surrounding websites is freer. "An editor of a newspaper or magazine has to make a conscious decision about what happens in his pages," says Wellings. "There is a lot of history on what has happened to publishers" who were sued, she adds. Because of the vastness of cyberspace, few screening mechanisms exist. "Imagine the bureaucracy of policing everything online," says Wellings. "An Internet service provider would have to go to great lengths and spend a lot of money." As a result, most ISPs maintain that they are merely a conduit for individuals who want to post information online. While most ISPs have policies telling people not to post offensive material, that warning is often ignored.

While some of what is published online may seem libelous, proving that point can be difficult and expensive. In order to prove libel, you have to prove malicious intent, something that might be difficult if the offending page was put up by an adolescent. And many times, freedom of speech wins out.

Unless an actual crime has taken place, law-enforcement officials often are unable to arrest anyone, even if they can identify the culprit. According to Lt. John Otero, commanding officer of the computer crime squad of the New York City Police Department, someone would actually have to post a threat in order for the police to act. "For example, if they say, tomorrow I am going to hurt, kill, or injure an individual, that would constitute a crime," he says. A person posting such a threat could be arrested and charged with aggravated harassment. Although Lieutenant Otero says his department has seen some arrests, anyone under eighteen years of age would not be dealt with harshly. "If the kid is too young, he would get a scolding and the incident would be brought to the parents' attention," he says. "If they are under sixteen, they are considered minors."

Most of what police departments see, however, does not constitute an actual crime. "What we get is a lot of 'he said, she said,' not unlike what you would find in the boys' room, only now they are doing it using electronics," says Lieutenant Otero.

While the cyberbully believes he or she cannot be caught, everyone leaves footprints in cyberspace. "Everything is traceable," says Loretta Radice, who taught computer skills to middle schoolers in public and private schools for more than fifteen years. Radice is now director and technology consultant for RADICEL Educational Technology Services, in New York, and holds private computer classes for children and adults. "Kids often don't realize that."

For example, anyone putting up a web page in cyberspace needs to pay with a credit card. If your child is being taunted online, you can type in the name of the website on www.whois.com, and find out who paid for the offending web page.

Similarly, e-mails and instant messages can be traced through screen names and addresses provided by the Internet service provider, such as America Online. Uncovering the culprit may take time, effort, and possibly even the help of a technology expert. But it can be done. Patti Kinney, principal of Talent Middle School in Talent, Oregon, and past president of the National Middle School Association, says that she will work with parents if their children are being harassed online. "If we can help, we will give it our best shot," she says. "If the incident is beyond our control, we will help them contact the police or an ISP."

"Sometimes bullying can be refuted because everything is verbal and there is no trail," says Beth Madison, principal of the George Middle School, in Portland, Oregon, in the January/February issue of *Our Children*. With cyberbullying, however, children can be taught to print out any offending messages. Madison says a girl in her school printed out offensive IMs. Armed with the evidence, her parents were able to come to school and have the administration intervene.

## The More Things Change . . .

The technology has changed. What hasn't changed, however, is that kindness and decency should still be top priorities for everyone. Vow to have an equal exchange with your daughter. Let her teach you about all those fancy gizmos you have bought her. You teach her about values. Encourage her to treat others the way she wants to be treated—the good old golden rule. No name-calling. No rumor-mongering. No excluding others. Here are some other things to consider.

**Emphasize privacy.** Help your daughter understand that not everything, particularly her sex life, needs to be made public. Perhaps the characters in *Sex and the City* confessed every last detail to their friends. She doesn't have to and shouldn't. Those confessions could very well end up on the Internet.

**Guard passwords.** Someone out to cause trouble can use another child's screen name to send out offensive e-mails. Tell your child not to share passwords with friends and to change passwords frequently.

**Keep copies.** Having documentation will strengthen your case if you need to report harassment to school or other au-

## HOW KIDS TEASE AND TORMENT
## USING NEW TECHNOLOGY

**Vicious e-mails.** "You've got mail" sometimes means "You've got insults," as mean kids use cyberspace to pass along verbal abuse, foul language, and hateful rumors.

**Insensitive IMs.** Instant messaging (being able to talk to another person on screen) can get nasty when the offending party uses this delivery system to spread hate and venom.

**Wicked websites.** Many web pages are creative and helpful. Some, however, have become gathering areas where kids can post vicious rumors and racist threats.

**Web logs (blogs).** Kids design these online journals to profile themselves and share their thoughts. Troublemakers, however, create these pages to ridicule, often morphing photos of the targeted victim into something ugly and humiliating.

**Cell phone photos.** In a cruel version of *Candid Camera,* the clueless victim is snapped during an embarrassing moment and the images are shared with everyone on the Internet.

**Text messaging.** Sending text messages via cell phone, bullies can reach out and touch a huge audience, spreading hurtful gossip along the way.

**Video cameras.** *America's Funniest Home Videos* becomes America's Cruelest Videos when these productions are edited for prime-time humiliation and broadcast over the Internet.

thorities. Lieutenant Otero advises that you should not delete the original e-mail, even after you have printed it out. "There may be something in the original header that would lead us to the source," he says.

**Report incidents.** If you think someone has broken a law, report the incident. Even if a crime has not been committed, take action in other directions. Contact your Internet service provider, other parents, anyone you think may know something or who could help.

**Do a technology check.** Does your daughter need to be so fully equipped? Does a ten-year-old really need a picture phone? Just because it comes with the deal doesn't mean she should have it. The device may create more problems than it's worth. Pass it up.

# CHAPTER 11

# Teach Your Children Well

*How Your Parenting Affects Your Daughter's Romantic Life*

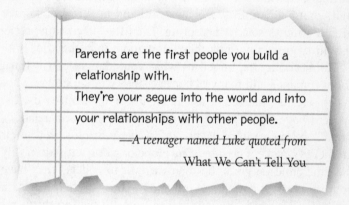

> Parents are the first people you build a relationship with.
> They're your segue into the world and into your relationships with other people.
>
> —*A teenager named Luke quoted from What We Can't Tell You*

A first kiss brushes a young girl's lips typically between the ages of ten and fifteen. It's one of those delicious firsts.

Girls are eager to know how to kiss. Can good kissing be taught? Is there a right way or a wrong way to lock lips? Twelve-year-olds have been known to practice on pillows. Movie make-outs serve as instructional preview. A very young Reese Witherspoon tries out her kissing technique in one of her earliest films, *The Man in the Moon*. A girl closes her eyes and tilts her face so as not to crash nose to nose with her fantasy kiss mate. Does she bend left or right?

Parents don't have to fret about kissing lessons. Young adolescents needn't bother with the practice sessions. Kissing comes instinctively. German professor of biopsychology Dr. Onur Güntürkün snuck a peek while 124 couples, aged thirteen to seventy, smooched. Sixty-five percent turned their heads to the right. Why? As it turns out, most people angle their face to the right, stemming from the same propensity that makes them right-handed, right-legged, right-eyed, or right-eared. Human beings are right-handed in a proportion of approximately eight to one.

Yes, when it comes to romantic behavior some things come naturally, but not all. When it comes to learning how to love well, young girls mostly feel awkward and unsure and so they need a parent's steady mentoring. Even the precocious, reckless, flirty girls only think they know more than they do.

Think about this: much of what your daughter will learn about romance and many of her decisions will depend on you. When Harris Interactive asked eight- to eighteen-year-olds, "Where have you learned the most about love and relationships?" 68 percent of eight- to twelve-year-olds said their mother; 47 percent credited Dad alone or along with Mom. "By the time children go off on their own, or to college, they have your ideas about dating and romance—you—in their heads," a mother of four kids, ranging in age from thirteen to thirty, reminded us.

With that romantic harbinger in mind, this chapter zeroes in on you and, more specifically, how your behavior, attitudes, and teachings—both conscious and unconscious—impact your daughters and how they love. We will repeat fascinating links that emerge between parents and adolescents in the arena of romantic history and adventures. If you are still one of those parents who doesn't want any dating under your roof (even after our dating advice) pay special attention to what's ahead. The "how" of your parenting style even goes as far as pinpointing what type of guy your little girl may pick as a boyfriend. Hopefully, the complexities of romantic role-modeling will become clearer.

In an episode of *Joan of Arcadia,* a TV family drama, Joan's father consoled his wife with the sentiment that parenting means getting hit with new stuff every day. Amen. All of us are learning as we go, and trying to get better at it.

## Caught in the Middle

You've read about how young adolescents labor under the weight of developmental deficits, namely hormones and puberty. Tweenagers are sometimes (although some days it seems like all the time), mean, moody, and miserable to live with. Living in bodies and being directed by brains undergoing growth spurts isn't easy. Ten- to fifteen-year-olds have a hard enough time dealing with life—their activities and schoolwork—much less navigating the murkier realm of their love lives. When girls start acting boy crazy, then obsessive, tumultuous, and confusing scripts begin to emerge.

When it comes to age-related deficits, adults rarely think of themselves as developmentally challenged. It just so happens that many forty-something moms are reaching perimenopause at the same time their daughters are hitting puberty. For an older mother, missing a period may bring panic: Could I be pregnant? During a hot flash she can feel incredibly sad with the realization that her childbearing years are about to end. A middle-aged female body loses estrogen, creating a host of side effects, including night sweats and loss of memory, to name a few. Irritability from out-of-whack hormones, sleeplessness, and fluctuating emotional temperatures—these mothers and their preteens have much in common. Over the slightest thing, both can become volatile, irritable, frustrated, depressed, forgetful, and weepy. Hear this: many mother-daughter pairs are destined to clash because of dueling hormones. Could we be talking about you? Or your spouse?

Aging mothers are vulnerable to bittersweet reactions over their daughters flowering into young, nubile women. A forty-five-year-old mother reminisced to us about this discovery while she and her daughter vacationed. She explained, "It was a hot day and we went into town dressed in sarongs over our bathing suits. I was jarred because the wolf whistles were aimed at my fifteen-year-old, not me. As proud as I felt of her, such a lovely creature attracting admiring eyes, my pride took a hit. It's not easy getting older. There's no competing with youth." Another woman, a former singer and the mother of a sixteen-year-old, told us, "My daughter sings better than I ever did, she's prettier than I ever was, smarter than I am, thinner than I am, and taller." Beneath her words gushed awe, admiration, and, yes, envy.

These ladies owned up to feelings that other, less candid women may suppress. Women in their thirties, forties, and fifties must adapt to aging while at the same time their daughters are becoming more sexual and attractive. Passing that baton of youth and beauty on to the younger generation is not easy. As mothers wrestle with whether to grow old gracefully or fight back with facial creams, Botox, and plastic surgery, these aftershocks affect how many handle their adolescent's social life.

In a culture that adores youth, older women carry baggage along with their crow's feet or sagging jowls. In a study of two hundred families with adolescents, mothers reported that when their child began to date they felt a significant increase in feelings of self-doubt, regret with regard to past decisions, and the desire to change the circumstances of their lives.

Men were not immune either. Fathers, especially of sons, felt the same, but expressed an added sense of confusion. On the one hand, they experienced more anxiety and depression. On the other hand, they felt flushes of high self-esteem attributed to vicarious pleasure at a son's social potency and pleasure.

A footnote of bad news emerged for their wives: fathers with sons or daughters with active social lives revealed lower levels of marital satisfaction. It seems women as mothers and wives get a double whammy of negatives.

According to one of the study's architects, Laurence Steinberg, "Seeing a child date calls forth a mixture of anxiety (over the adolescent's sexuality), envy (over the adolescent's freedom), regret (over the romantic choices one didn't pursue), and longing (for one's youth)." They conclude that these collective reactions, or dissatisfactions, can set the stage for battles and bickering with teens.

Could this explain a tantrum at a dance recaptured by a school counselor? She said, "I watched this father create a scene at our school mixer. His daughter was freak dancing, which involved her grinding up against her partner. I admit it looked suggestive, but I've seen far worse. He stormed onto the dance floor and literally pulled the tween away from a very surprised boy. I couldn't catch his words exactly but his drift was obvious. I overheard the girl interrupting him in desperate tones with 'Dad, it doesn't mean anything.' Vehemently he shouted above thumping DJ sounds, 'It does mean something! Especially in the middle of an open, public place.' "

Parents need to set boundaries, to be sure, and to draw lines about behavior that they deem inappropriate. However, if you hear yourself shouting about your daughter's clothing, or when you catch her kissing on the couch, bite your tongue. Pubescent and teenage behavior triggers a parent's personal demons with regard to aging and sexuality. The point of the research, and the implication of this anecdote, suggests what murky territory monitoring can be for parents.

## Conduct Unbecoming a Romantic Role Model

In 2003 the National Campaign to Prevent Teen Pregnancy asked kids to tell them who they looked to for instruction on good relationships. For healthy, responsible relationship role modeling, 59 percent of the adolescents surveyed claimed that parents' behavior taught them what they wanted to learn.

That our marriages and divorces, rapprochements and fights serve as "romance lessons" for the majority of our children is a sobering realization. If you look into the mirror and wince at the vivid memory of last week's fight or an ongoing stalemate, you are hardly alone. If you wither, convinced that your divorce has ruined your daughter's chances of ever having a happy, lasting marriage, don't despair. Few of us have perfect marriages, sublime second (or third) marriages, or smooth, peaceful divorces. Quit emotionally laden finger-pointing and focus on some documented truths as you examine your role-modeling conscience.

Let's address divorce guilt first. Books have come down the pike condemning children of divorce to a lifetime of gloom, wounds, and marital doom. That forecast has been disputed by psychologist E. Mavis Hetherington, whose findings stem from the Virginia Longitudinal Study of Divorce, the most comprehensive ever of 1,400 families over three decades. Unlike many previous surveys, this one contrasted the families of divorce with a control group. In Hetherington's book, *For Better or For Worse: Divorce Reconsidered,* she delivers good news to divorced mothers of girls.

Most girls survive parents' marital meltdown perfectly well. Hetherington points out, "Although they looked back on their parents' breakup as a painful experience, most were successfully going about the tasks of young adulthood: establishing careers, creating intimate relationships, building meaningful lives for themselves." Some girls actually flourished by becoming exceptionally confident and competent.

What makes or breaks post-divorce families? "To a great extent," says Hetherington, "individuals determine their own destiny." When a divorced single mother focuses on her own personal growth, when she structures positive goals for herself and works toward meeting them, she sets a powerful example of resilience.

If dealing with the former spouse poses problems, here are two suggestions that may enhance a daughter's well-being. Minimize contact with an ex if the two of you can't get along, but make sure that your spouse stays in contact with his daughter, because girls fare better when fathers remain in their lives. Take special note of this fact: research shows that fathers favor boys, retaining a better post-divorce contact schedule with sons.

Next, what about negotiating conflict within a marriage and a family? Fighting in front of children, and how destructive it can be, constitutes a recurring theme in magazine articles and on TV talk shows. In all honesty, who among us, married or in a long-term romantic relationship, hasn't gotten into a fight with a mate? Or yelled at family members? Eighty-eight percent of 991 families fessed up to verbal ballistics aimed at their children, *The Journal of Marriage and Family* reported in 2003.

"Marriage is a disagreement machine," insists Diane Sollee, founder of Coalition for Marriage, Family, and Couples Education in Washington, DC, in *Psychology Today*. "Every couple has about ten 'irreconcilable differences'—who to vote for, what church to go to, how much money to save. All couples disagree about all the same things. We have a highly romanticized notion that if we were the right person, we wouldn't fight."

Experts who have analyzed conflict contend that everyone tends to argue about four basic issues, namely money, sex, kids, and leisure. Even more telling, though, is what psychologist and author of *The Seven Principles for Making Marriage Work* John Gottman has discovered. Divorced spouses and couples married for years have the same numbers of blowups. There's virtually no difference. How come? People in committed relationships before, during, and after marriage disagree. It's not the fact that they fight, or how often, that counts, but how they resolve their differences and the issues.

Many scholars have developed models for helping couples learn how to argue and resolve conflicts. One such program, from New York University's Child Studies Center, warns couples to avoid common traps. File their suggestions for your own benefit:

- Don't resort to sarcasm.
- Don't let arguments escalate until you are too angry to communicate in a civil way.

- Don't shut down. Neither should one partner withdraw and refuse to talk.
- Refrain from disparaging insults.
- Don't jump to conclusions. Assuming the worst or trying to read someone's mind rarely works.
- Keep one issue on the table at a time. Don't lump all your gripes into one conflict session as in "You won't do this and I hate your mother, and . . ." Digesting one issue, one argument at a time, is workout enough for a couple. The weight of too many critiques will squash the most committed souls.

The behavior most unbecoming a role model, the misbehavior most threatening, is family violence and domestic abuse. In chapter 4, we noted how frequently young adolescents tolerate emotional and physical abuse, and how confusing the definitions and boundaries have become to them. If your marriage contains elements of emotional and/or physical abuse, whether you are victim or victimizer, you create a legacy that becomes familiar and, chances are, will be passed down to your children. Consult a family therapist if you have doubts.

Spend extra time teaching your children how to avoid this family history. In *The Date Rape Prevention Book,* crime prevention specialist Scott Lindquist advocates that parents preach assertiveness. "Assertiveness is the ability to exercise one's own rights while respecting the rights of others. Help your teen learn the difference between passive, assertive, and aggressive behavior."

All parents need to work extra hard at creating a healthy example of real-life relationships, of warts-and-all working marriages. From a variety of experts, we have gleaned some guiding principles.

**Live by illustrating compromise.** When two people wed, they will disagree. Each one wins some of the time and loses some of the time. A give-and-take rhythm should be obvious in decision making. Married life and committed relationships are shared ventures, not dictatorships.

**Talk and treat each other with respect.** You can still fight so long as you behave at all times with civility. Choose "I" rather than language that blames or name-calls. For example, "I feel overwhelmed when you don't help me with housework." Not "You are a lazy, selfish bum for assuming every chore around this place is my job."

In the November 9, 2004, *New York Times,* Dr. Murray Straus, director of the Family Research Laboratory at the University of New Hampshire, underscored the dangerous ripple effect of uncontrolled raised voices, "Yelling sets the tone for family relationships . . . that [tone can] carry over into dating relationships where you get a lot of psychological aggression."

**Support each other.** This is easy when you agree or share a goal. However, support really counts when one partner wants to espouse an opinion or pursue a hobby or goal that the other partner doesn't share or approve of. Yet such tolerance underscores the basic truth that couples are made up of individuals. Acknowledge and respect your partner's wishes.

**Freedom belongs in a healthy relationship.** Partners can have separate friends. Relationships or activities outside a marriage do not destroy or betray the marital bond. Positive partners don't try to control one another, but allow freedom.

**Put jealousy into perspective.** When it pops up, address the issue of trust. Choose trust over jealousy.

None of us will live up to these relationship values all the time. However, when we fall short we can apologize (preferably in front of the children). Spouses can recommit themselves to the behaviors and sentiments that will make a union last. In so doing, we model the benefits of healthy relationships to our kids, who are our audience every day.

## What's Your Parenting Style?

So far in this book, we've introduced you to different kinds of parents. We've portrayed the hysterically terrified parent who is convinced that the first kiss is the kiss of death. Then we warned of the too-permissive kind who misguidedly hosts the after-prom party and serves alcohol to minors. You've met parents who are in the same throes of dating as their adolescent daughters, who can critique their dates over milk and cookies at midnight. You've seen parents who panic at the first glimpse of a girl's belly bared, in comparison with others who push their girls to become popular princesses in middle school.

How would you characterize the way you in particular govern your daughter's social behavior and romantic initiatives? Are you strict? Does your anxiety tend to make you fall on the rigid side when it comes to letting her wear a sexy outfit or attend a rock or hip-hop concert? Or do you pride yourself on giving your daughter freedom, say to show off her newfound curves or accompany friends to hear a controversial music artist live? If so, how do you decide how much freedom is too much? Do you feel shut out of your adolescent's life and therefore feel you are not in the loop to exert any influence on her fate?

No one ever said that raising an adolescent was easy, much less one on the cusp of socializing and falling in love. Since most of us need all the help available, consider how your parenting style affects your child. Actually much has been written on the standard ways that mothers and fathers, stepparents and grandparents parent the children in their care. Experts divide parents into categories depending upon the way they set boundaries and delegate power to children.

Here is a roundup review of the typical types of parents: the authoritarian, the authoritative, the absentee, and the friend-parents, which is one category that we have added.

**Authoritarian parents** firmly believe that they know best and, consequently, formulate strict rules. They view their family as a hierarchy with Mom and Dad in the ruling position.

Obedience figures prominently. When a child deviates from family values, the parents exact rigid consequences, usually punishments.

**Authoritative parents** are attentive to what's happening in the lives of their children. They monitor, but they differ from the first type in that they believe raising children is a joint venture. To their way of thinking, families are more of a democracy. They allow, and even encourage, their children to voice their opinions and share in decision making. They have rules and try to be consistent. However, they make room for flexibility and a child's point of view.

**Absentee parents** are not in tune or in touch with the lives of their children. If there are rules, they are haphazardly enforced. These mothers and fathers range from being overwhelmed to being self-absorbed. The underlying cause of the absence could be that their lives are spinning out of control from divorce, family crisis, or illness, or that the parent has chosen work above family.

In our experience with parents over the last decade we have identified another type that needs to be mentioned.

**Friend-parents** are mothers or fathers who are confused about the boundary between being the adult and the teen. They prefer to think of themselves and their tweenage and teenage offspring as equals. They are uncomfortable with being in charge.

Children have friends and they don't need parents to behave as if they are in that category.

Most parents (though not all), regardless of parenting style, want the best for their offspring. In all categories there may be good intentions, but they are not enough.

The attitudes and leeway that parents hold and permit significantly affect ten- to fifteen-year-olds. Since tweens normally battle for independence and yearn to explore new ideas and launch new adventures, some parenting styles are healthier than others; some create more fireworks than others.

In families where the mothers and fathers willingly and warmly listen and share power, adolescents perform better in school and more successfully ward off the temptations surrounding these risk-taking years. This authoritative style creates closeness and increases a rapport that seems to create a safety net around tweens. This safety net protects kids from delinquency and alcohol and substance abuse.

In the realm of decision making, an interesting link has been suggested, compliments of a study published in the *Journal of Research on Adolescence*. According to the investigation of psychologists D. L. Durbin, N. Darling, L. Steinberg, and B. B. Brown, kids who described their parents as authoritative were more likely to choose for friends well-rounded peers who share the values of their parents. They opted to socialize with the "brains" and "populars." Adolescents who judged their parents to be uninvolved, picked peers who rejected adult norms. These kids were drawn to rebel groups such as the "druggies."

So if your daughter wants to hang with types who spell trouble and if she opts for the bad boys or the wild ones, you should sit down with your spouse and analyze your parenting style. Could she be rebelling or acting out in response to a too-strict or a too-lenient family discipline style? Simplistic, perhaps, but worth considering if you are distressed over the boys your daughter falls for or the fast crowd with whom she wants to run.

Those parent types who are *not* flexible and *not* inclined to release power and control—the authoritarian ones—risk more tension and arguments over social and romantic choices. Conversely, mothers and fathers who willingly encourage autonomy and respect a child's rights to her own feelings and opinions have a built-in advantage. They provide the context to permit a range of good and not-so-good choices. They tend to have fewer arguments, and these tweens are more likely to learn from bad decisions. When it comes to guiding a young adolescent, parents would be advised to embrace the style of parenting that combines monitoring with shared power. And, let us add, always remember that you are the adult.

Finally, remember those errors parents often made, the Oops top ten (see pages 8–16)? In order to refresh your memory and demonstrate how far you can go, we've turned the mistakes around. Here are ten affirmations.

1. Empathize with your daughter, even the very young "puppy lover," about the highs and lows she may be experiencing.

2. Recognize that your daughter's romantic readiness happens before you may be ready. Embrace her capacity to love.

3. Know when to be a hands-on supervisor and a hands-off monitor of her romances. Practice reserve.

4. Keep a respectful distance from her boyfriends. Never flirt with them.

5. You and your husband should construct your rules and your restrictions as a united front. If you have a blended family with a mix of ex-spouses and stepparents, do your best to see that the same rules apply from household to household.

6. Hold your tongue after a dance, social event, or date. It's a good idea to be awake and attentive when your child comes in after a social occasion. A hug and a kiss may be in order too if you suspect alcohol experimentation. Getting close will allow you to smell alcohol on a child's breath. Your daughter will share information in her own time.

7. Respect her privacy. Be honest. Trust her (until she gives you reason not to). This trio will give you what you need to know about your daughter's love life and well-being. Snooping or interrogating friends won't.

8. Share your romantic memories and experiences. Give her the opportunity to create her own unique memories.

9. Create house rules, have talks about sex, and cultivate fam-

ily values that are the same for all the boys and girls in your family.

10. Capitalize on every window of opportunity.

As a parent you are a profound and pivotal partner in your daughter's love life. You may not always ask the right questions. You may not even have all the answers. Be mindful of your own behavior and your powerful romantic role-modeling. Through crushes and broken hearts, kiss your child. And remind her that you always love her. Your mom probably said that whenever you got hurt. Back then you may have thought it was small consolation. But if you can still hear "I love you, no matter what," then the words offered more consolation than you thought at the time.

## Epilogue I: An Encore . . . More Oops

Remember, guiding your young adolescent never ends. There will always be opportunities for healing her wounds and defusing her woes. For a parent, though, there's always room for making new mistakes. Here's a heads-up on ten more.

**1. Don't assume that you are the best teacher.** Rightfully, a parent wants to be the one to govern the romantic values and sexual ethics that a daughter lives by. Despite your strong feelings about this, some adolescents believe that their love lives are not a parent's business. (We heard this sentiment ourselves from teens.) Such kids, especially older teens who may be involved in sexual activity, feel more comfortable talking to someone— anyone—other than a mother or father. So encourage your tweens to develop rapport with others: a favorite aunt, a family physician, a school counselor, a gynecologist or a stepparent. It does take a village sometimes to get a tweenager through.

**2. Resist the urge to talk too much.** Beware of this tendency, especially after you close the pages of our book. We hope you will feel motivated to talk, talk, talk. At the risk of sounding like we are contradicting ourselves, we want you to chill. Not every conversation needs to be a romance training session. Not every television show, every movie, every music video should spur you into a "What do you think about this?" Q&A. Sometimes small talk should just be that. Even when you chat about nothing significant, you and your daughter deepen your rapport and increase the odds that she will see you as a confidante.

**3. Delay denying your permission.** Ten- to fifteen-year-olds hear "no" a great deal. Many want to push the limits of curfews and crash through the boundaries of where they can go alone or what they are allowed to do. Stretch out your "no's." For example, your seventh-grader wants to go out to a party with her older brother, a party where older teens will be. She asks, "Can I?" Don't say no immediately. Instead offer, "Let me think about that." In the meantime, she may think about what could happen there, the good and the bad. When you bring down the ax and offer the reasons why, she may fight you less.

**4. Don't exclusively knock sexy idols and edgy icons.** MTV Hits, FUSE, VH-1, the red carpet before the Grammys or the Oscars—endless examples of lewd lyrics, indecent clothing, and obscene dance moves beg for your criticism. So as not to seem 100 percent negative, look for positive examples among icons and idols. Admire the style of songstresses who dress (dare we say) modestly for the red carpet. Compliment artists who showcase their talent, and not only their flesh, in music videos. (Alicia Keys comes to mind.) Admit that you love a particular star, but not everything he or she is known for.

**5. Don't "freak out" when you learn your daughter has engaged in sex.** It's natural to feel disappointed, angry, or sad if you find out that your child has had oral sex or intercourse with her boyfriend. Let your emotional reactions settle before addressing sexual issues with her. Chances are that she does need some guidance to make sense of, or understand fully, why she did what she did. Where does she go from here? A girl must learn to feel comfortable with her sexual decisions. She has to decide whether to have sex again with the next partner. Put your comfort level aside, and help her move on with more insight into her future sexual decisions. She may decide postponing sex proved right after all.

**6. Don't leave your spouse out on movie night.** When you watch old movies and reminisce about which stars caught your fancy and figured in your fantasies, include your spouse. Let him chime in on Mrs. Robinson or Marilyn Monroe. If you start to feel jealous, shelve that envy for now. It's more important to include Dad, as too many fathers do not participate in conversations about love.

**7. Never violate a daughter's confidence.** Trust is highly valued by tweens. Suppose your daughter tells you that a girlfriend of hers has had sexual intercourse. Suppose she confesses that one of her friends has had oral sex with three boys in the last month. You know the girl, and her mother. You waver: What's the right thing to do? On the one hand, you don't want to be the bearer of scandalous news. On the other, if your daughter were going too far you would want to know, right?

Whatever your daughter tells you in confidence, you need to honor. If you go behind her back and reveal her confidence, she will find out. Her friends will be furious with her. Bottom line: your child will not trust you in the future. In our book on privacy issues, a majority of young adolescents said that they would be more honest with their parents if those parents would keep their confidences. So be trustworthy. If you are convinced that you need to let an adult in on a girl's sexual behavior, discuss your intended action with your daughter first. Explain why you need to make that call. Another option is to tell your daughter you want to confide with a school counselor. In that way, the girl deep in sexual territory can be approached sensitively by a qualified adult, not by a parent who might punish her.

**8. Don't let mean girls off the hook, even when they are good girls most of the time.** There may be times when your daughter's circle of friends turn on her. One makes a hurtful remark or sends a nasty e-mail. Another excludes her from a sleepover. Your daughter feels crushed. What advice do you give? This is incredibly sticky. First of all, you like your daughter's girlfriends for the most part. They are basically nice. Furthermore, you know that tomorrow they may apologize or act like no mean words or deeds ever happened. Nevertheless, you need to call a spade a spade. Tell your daughter that their behavior is cruel and wrong. When the girls get around to making up, including your child again, advise your daughter to address their wrongs. Let her remind them that friends do not hurt friends. You may not be able to erase mean behavior from all girl-to-girl interactions during the tween years, but you can underline it and condemn it. To do otherwise confuses your daughter. Furthermore, she may conclude, inaccurately, that you care less about her feelings than her popularity.

**9. Don't let your sons act disrespectfully toward girls.** Your adolescent son calls his ex-girlfriend a nasty name (slut, bitch). Or he and his friends sit in front of the TV leering and snickering, making obscene comments about someone, say Anna Nicole Smith. Don't let this behavior pass as "boys will be boys." During these years, tween girls are extremely vigilant about picking up on what others think and say and believe. They are also looking to see if boys get away with more. If you want your daughters to avoid stereotyping and bad-mouthing, you must set the same standard for your sons.

**10. Don't participate in gossip about whether or not someone is gay, lesbian, or bisexual.** The tabloids frequently run stories about celebrities being secretly homosexual. Is Tom Cruise gay? This same kind of innuendo happens to any number of kids during middle school. When speculation starts about a celebrity, say, "Is it our business?" When you overhear the "is she or isn't she?" conversation about a young adolescent peer, ask: "Why does it matter?" Or say, "I have always liked Katlin and still feel that way whether she is gay or not." Middle school rumor mills work 24/7 and sexual identity issues figure prominently. If your daughter is worried about a friend or herself, that is a different matter. Then talk things through.

We'll remind you once more that there are no perfect parents and no perfect kids. Give each other slack and forgiveness.

## Epilogue 2

A healthy interest in boys can snowball. A girl can become too boy crazy. In case you need a gauge, we invite you to use the following test as a resource.

## Is Your Daughter Boy Crazy?

How much boy talk is too much? Take a time-out with this test and see where your daughter registers on the scale of boy-crazy behavior.

Directions: This is a multiple-choice test. Read each statement or question carefully. Choose one answer, even if you have to guesstimate. Then proceed to the scoring section.

1. What does makeup mean to your daughter? _____
    a) Too much, she wants to wear eye shadow, mascara, lipstick to school every day. We battle because I think it's inappropriate for her age

b) An occasional dress-up game is the way my daughter perceives makeup

c) She's begun experimenting with glitter and lip gloss but isn't pushing for more

2. How do you characterize your daughter's physical development? _____

a) She is just beginning to blossom with budding breasts and slight curves

b) My daughter is classic early puberty, the first in her class to develop breasts and hips

c) My baby still looks like a little girl compared to many in her class

3. The middle school rumor mill _____

a) is not really on my child's radar so far as I can tell

b) is an ongoing who's-going-out-with-whom conversation among my child and her friends

c) has had more than one round with my daughter playing the starring romantic lead

4. Do clothes make your girl? _____

a) My daughter likes to shop at the mall and buy a bit of the latest fashion fads

b) My daughter is a little label conscious, but doesn't give clothes too much thought

c) My daughter is very fashion conscious and wants to dress like a sexy model or rock star

5. To your child, a party is _____

a) like the air she breathes and she's always planning one or going to one

b) an occasional boy-girl event revolving around a birthday or bar mitzvah

c) a sleepover with her girlfriends

6. Where does your daughter fit in the middle school social hierarchy? _____

a) She's just an ordinary kid with a few friends

b) She is very popular and hangs with the in-crowd

c) She is very tuned in to who the coolest kids are and longs to be accepted by that group

7. If you hear suddenly that tweens in your community filmed and starred in their own X-rated video playing on the Internet _____
   a) your response would include panic because you fear that your daughter would be involved in a featured role
   b) your response would be curiosity, but you'd make no connection between the scandal and your child
   c) you would be very curious and talk to your daughter about who's involved and how this happened

8. Does your daughter have a boyfriend? _____
   a) If a crush on someone qualifies then yes
   b) She's had one or two but they only last a few weeks
   c) A boyfriend? how about a list of boys that changes faster than I can keep track of?

9. Has your daughter's schoolwork been affected by her socializing? _____
   a) A little bit, she's not as focused as before
   b) Not at all
   c) Definitely, academics are at the bottom of her priority list

10. Which description most closely fits your child's social life? _____
    a) My daughter runs with a fast and popular crowd
    b) My daughter socializes a lot, goes to the mall and movies with a mixed group
    c) My daughter has a few good friends and their lives seem to revolve around sports, music, or some other common interest.

11. On the subject of dating: _____
    a) It hasn't come up
    b) It causes fights because my daughter thinks she's old enough to go out alone with a boy and I disagree
    c) My daughter goes out in a group, but I wouldn't call this dating

12. Do you suspect that your daughter has tried alcohol? _____

a) Yes
b) No
c) I'm not sure

13. Has the disturbing thought that your daughter is experimenting with sex crossed your mind more than once? _____

   a) No, maybe a kiss but nothing more
   b) Not my daughter, but I do think one of her friends is doing sexual stuff
   c) Honestly, I am worried especially about oral sex

14. What do you make of your daughter's pop, hip-hop, or rock idols? _____
   a) My daughter and her friends are definitely bonding over the latest musical stars. They watch TRL and listen to the same artists.
   b) I find my daughter's musical taste interesting so long as I don't have to listen to it all the time
   c) My daughter's music favorites worry me because they murmur sexual lyrics and writhe in scanty outfits, and she sees nothing wrong with it

15. When you eavesdrop on your daughter interacting with her peers, you mostly hear _____
   a) Who is doing what with whom, and your imagination is working overtime
   b) Who's hot and who's going out with whom
   c) Who's not talking to whom and why

Scoring: List all of your answers in the space provided. Then look to see which points apply. Write in your points in the space provided, then total your score. Then proceed to what your score means.

|  |  |  | Answer | Points |
|---|---|---|---|---|
| 1. (a) 15 | (b) 5 | (c) 10 | ___ | ___ |
| 2. (a) 10 | (b) 15 | (c) 5 | ___ | ___ |
| 3. (a) 5 | (b) 10 | (c) 15 | ___ | ___ |

|       | (a)  | (b)  | (c)  |     |     |
|-------|------|------|------|-----|-----|
| 4.    | (a) 10 | (b) 5  | (c) 15 | ___ | ___ |
| 5.    | (a) 15 | (b) 10 | (c) 5  | ___ | ___ |
| 6.    | (a) 5  | (b) 15 | (c) 10 | ___ | ___ |
| 7.    | (a) 15 | (b) 10 | (c) 5  | ___ | ___ |
| 8.    | (a) 5  | (b) 10 | (c) 15 | ___ | ___ |
| 9.    | (a) 10 | (b) 5  | (c) 15 | ___ | ___ |
| 10.   | (a) 15 | (b) 10 | (c) 5  | ___ | ___ |
| 11.   | (a) 5  | (b) 15 | (c) 10 | ___ | ___ |
| 12.   | (a) 15 | (b) 5  | (c) 10 | ___ | ___ |
| 13.   | (a) 5  | (b) 10 | (c) 15 | ___ | ___ |
| 14.   | (a) 10 | (b) 5  | (c) 15 | ___ | ___ |
| 15.   | (a) 15 | (b) 10 | (c) 5  | ___ | ___ |

Total Points _____

## Evaluation

**75–100 points—*Boys are not high on her radar*** If your score fell in this range, even though you may hear giggles and see her gawk, your daughter is not ready for boys yet. Her definition of a party is a sleepover. You may have found her rummaging through your cosmetics case, but it's no more than a tweenage version of dress-up. When your child gets dressed, shops at the mall, chats with her friends, or does her homework, none of these activities are boy-driven as in *Will he like how I look?* or *Will he be intimidated by my better grades?* For now, you do not have to fret about the possibility of your little girl getting into sexually charged situations. "Boy crazy" does not describe your daughter, but prepare yourself, as romance and boys will show up on her radar in the future.

**105–165 points—*Boys are in the picture*** If your score fell in this range, your daughter is focused on boys, but not to the extreme. If you eavesdrop you will hear lots of gossip about who's going out with whom, who's popular and who's not cool. Chances are your little girl is beginning to dress more like a teenager and dabbing her face with gloss and glitter. She's dabbling in the party scene on occasion and going out in mixed groups. All of this is normal and healthy. That said, you still need to keep tuned in to her romantic blossoming because there may be temptation to try alcohol or engage in risky sexual behavior around the corner. There's a lot for a girl to learn and her friends are not the best teachers.

**170–225 points—*Boys are her main focus*** If your score fell in this range, your daughter is too preoccupied with boys. Your instinct has been telling you this. You are already on alert that a school scandal or a sexual entanglement might involve your child. Her grades have dropped in direct proportion to her interest in socializing and being part of the in-crowd. You've had arguments more than once over how much makeup she uses or what kind of clothes she wants to wear. She wants to look like the stars she sees on music television, the scantily clad and provocatively posed sexy sirens. Don't despair. Because now that you recognize that she's too focused on boys, you can guide her toward achieving more balance in her life.

# Index

# About the Authors

**Charlene C. Giannetti** is a journalist and the author of nine previous books, including *Who Am I? . . . And Other Questions of Adopted Kids*. She and her husband have a son and a daughter and live in New York City.

**Margaret Sagarese** is a former teacher, an educational materials writer, and the author of fourteen books. She lives on Long Island, New York, with her husband and daughter.